This book is due on the last date stamped below.
Failure to return books on the date due may result
in assessment of overdue fees.

LABOR AND WORKPLACE ISSUES IN LITERATURE

LABOR AND WORKPLACE ISSUES IN LITERATURE

Claudia Durst Johnson

Exploring Social Issues through Literature

GREENWOOD PRESS
Westport, Connecticut • London

Library of Congress Cataloging-in-Publication Data

Johnson, Claudia D.
   Labor and workplace issues in literature / Claudia Durst Johnson.
      p. cm.—(Exploring social issues through literature, ISSN 1551–0263)
   Includes bibliographical references and index.
   ISBN 0–313–33286–X
   1. American fiction—History and criticism. 2. Work in literature. 3. English prose
literature—History and criticism. 4. Terkel, Studs, 1912– Working. 5. Working class in
literature. I. Title. II. Series.
   PS374.W64J64   2006
   810.9'355—dc22   2005025974

British Library Cataloguing in Publication Data is available.

Library of Congress Catalog Card Number: 2005025974
ISBN: 0–313–33286–X
ISSN: 1551–0263

First published in 2006

Greenwood Press, 88 Post Road West, Westport, CT 06881
An imprint of Greenwood Publishing Group, Inc.
www.greenwood.com

Printed in the United States of America

The paper used in this book complies with the
Permanent Paper Standard issued by the National
Information Standards Organization (Z39.48–1984).

10 9 8 7 6 5 4 3 2 1

Contents

Series Foreword

Exploring Social Issues through Literature was developed as a resource to help teachers and librarians keep pace with secondary school curriculum developments in the language arts such as integrated studies and teaching literature across the curriculum. Each volume in the open-ended series confronts an important social issue that has both historical ramifications and contemporary relevance to high school students. The initial topics developed for the series reflect the "hot button" issues most requested by educators. Themes—such as environmental issues, bioethics, and racism—encompass a considerable body of literature. The books in this series provide readers with an introduction to the topic and examine the differing perspectives offered by authors and writers from a variety of time periods and literary backgrounds.

This resource was developed to address students' needs and appeal to their interests. The literary works selected range from standard canonical works to contemporary and multicultural adult fiction that would be familiar to teens and to young adult fiction. Many titles are found on curriculum reading lists; other considerations in selection include pertinence, interest level, subject and language appropriateness, and availability and accessibility of the text to the nonspecialist. The authors of these volumes, all experts in their fields, also sought to include a wide spectrum of works offering as many differing perspectives on the issue as possible.

Each volume begins with an introductory essay tracing the historical and literary developments related to the identified social issue. The chapters provide brief biographical information on the writer and present critical analysis of one or more work of literature. While the focus of the chapters is generally full-length fiction, it is not limited to that and may also include poetry, short stories, or nonfiction—such as essays or memoirs. In most chapters works are arranged chronologically to reflect the historical trends and developments. In other cases works are grouped according to thematic subtopics. The analysis includes discussions of the work's structural, thematic, and stylistic components and insights on the historical context that relates the work to the broader issue. Chapters conclude with bibliographic information on works cited and a list of suggested readings that may be helpful for further research or additional assignments.

Educators looking for new ways to present social issues will find this resource quite valuable for presenting thematic reading units or historical perspectives on modern problems of conflict. Students of literature as well as general readers will find many ideas and much inspiration in this series.

Introduction

"U.S. Pursues Forced Labor Case in Florida"
—*New York Times*, June 11, 2005

"Exec's Salaries Increased More Than Twice as Fast as Employees"
—*The Wall Street Journal*, May 29, 2005

"Heat Stroke Poses Ever-Present Farmworkers Peril"
—*West County Times*, August 22, 2004

"Can't Win for Losing: A Report from the World of 35 Million People Who Are not Making It in America"
—*New York Times Book Review*, February 15, 2004

It seems strange to find these headlines in what many regard as an enlightened age, a time when the public takes for granted worker protections put in place by the New Deal and trade union reforms. The persistence of outrages in agriculture and industry make the present study of labor and workplace issues in literature an especially timely one. An overview of the history of work is apt preparation for the in-depth scrutiny of labor that follows. Turning to the authoritative *Oxford English Dictionary* for definitions, one finds nine pages on the word *work* alone. The first, preferred definition is "something to be done or something to do" or "a particular act, a task or job" (V. 2, p. 286), "to act; to perform, practice a deed, course of action, labor, task" (289).

Labor has a slightly different connotation: "physical work esp. performed with the object of gaining a livelihood" (V. 2, p. 6). A *laborer* is described as "one who performs physical labour as a service or for a livelihood" (p. 7). The term *laborer* is seldom applied to the owner of a business or a member of a profession.

The creation of a product requires three elements. Labor is one of them. Capital, contributed by owners and stock holders, is another. A third is the raw material needed for production—lumber, iron, coal, or wool, for instance. Opinions about which element is most essential are at the heart of economic theory. The businessperson, naturally, sees capital as of first importance. The socialist ranks human labor first.

THE NEOLITHIC REVOLUTION

In looking at work theoretically, one encounters diametrically opposed attitudes toward it. Is it a curse or a blessing? A burdensome necessity or a means of self-fulfillment? A punishment or gift? An imposition or the way to self-identity? Stories about work are as old as civilization itself. "In the beginning," according to the key story of the Garden of Eden, expounded in the Old Testament, work was a curse. One thing that made Paradise perfect was the absence of work, and part of humankind's punishment for disobeying God was to be doomed forever to a life of toil. When God banishes Adam and Eve, they are informed that they now must "toil ... all the days of your life." (Genesis 3:17).

A second story, of Adam and Eve's sons, Cain and Abel, in the fourth chapter of Genesis, implies what has been labeled the Neolithic Revolution. When God demands sacrifices of the two men, Abel, the seminomadic hunter and sheep herder, offers up an animal. Cain, a "tiller of the ground," offers a gift of vegetable produce. After God refuses to accept Cain's vegetable offering, garnered through his work, but accepts Abel's gift, Cain, in a fit of jealous rage, kills his brother. The story of Cain and Abel—one a hunter and herder, the other a farmer—calls to mind the upheaval in the history of labor, coming at the end of the Stone Age and designated the Neolithic Revolution. Primitives were nomads, constantly on the move in search of game and edible flora. The Neolithic Revolution occurred when nomadic hunters and gatherers began remaining in one place to establish permanent homes, plant their own gardens, and domesticate animals. To survive, these early humans had to build shelters, forage for food, hunt, and protect themselves. As civilization advanced, some work became more complex, stratified, and specialized. As early as Homer, we find references to horse-breakers, pig-raisers, caretakers, soldiers, and court singers. In departure from earlier practices, families less often provided all of their own needs. A system of trades appeared, and people chose the more specialized work of weavers, blacksmiths, potters, carpenters, and so on. As trades developed, so did professions, devoted to single facets of work in areas of religion, medicine, and education.

Inevitably, a few gained ascendancy over the majority. Deep chasms separated a few powerful rulers from the great mass of workers. The privileged few had the right to own legally the labor of those who worked. Ancient Egyptian royalty owned the labor of many who worked as laborers and farmers, and the Romans owned the labor of those of other nations whom they had captured, forcing many into soldiering. In England, the manorial system evolved, whereby the excessive affluence of one family living in a great manor on hundreds of acres was created by an army of serfs living in hovels.

In the Western tradition, after the Protestant Reformation, work was *theoretically* no longer considered a curse, but a God-bestowed gift. Though in theory, all work—vocations—were honored in the Christian church's system of callings, an individual was confined to a lifetime of work suitable only to the social station into which he or she was born. So, for instance, a poor young man born into a family of serfs was forbidden by religion and the law from attempting to rise above the station into which he was born to become a clerk or a teacher. One clear case of how the doctrine of callings worked is seen in the life of John Bunyan, religious dissenter and author of *Pilgrim's Progress,* one of the most widely read and influential books of all times. The lowly born Bunyan, originally a tinker by trade, was considered to have violated God's design for him by daring to preach and write, jobs that were "above his station."

From the Reformation onward, idleness had been considered one of the worst of sins. Still, dogma was used to justify a class of people who never worked but lived in luxury from the work of others. God had given them high status from birth. He intended for them to be leaders, and for the lowly born to be followers.

As early as the fifteenth century, the small farmer experienced difficulties when some of the land, which was claimed by the aristocracy, but had been used in common to grow crops, began to be "enclosed" as grazing and hunting land for the landlords' sole use. This created another class of idle people, this time at the other end of the social spectrum: farmers who could no longer use the common tillage often became beggars. *Their* idleness, of course, was decidedly condemned.

Enclosure was still not widespread or universal until the mid-eighteenth century, at which time it became epidemic. Between 1761 and 1801 alone, 2,000 enclosure acts were passed by Parliament (whose members were made up of landed aristocracy).

THE INDUSTRIAL REVOLUTION

The most dramatic, defining event in economic history began in England in the eighteenth century and moved to the United States and Europe in the nineteenth century. This was called the Industrial Revolution. Literally, it was the replacement of manual labor with machines. It came about from, and was distinguished by, several circumstances. First, there were new advances in technology that radically changed the way in which goods were produced. It was also defined by improved communication, transportation, and new concepts of efficiency. Machines that were once run primarily by water were now powered by steam as a result of numerous inventions, notably that of James Watts, who harnessed steam power for use in factories, not just in mines. Even as early as 1709, a process was invented for converting coal to coke to produce iron and other metals. In 1784, a new way was developed for "rolling iron," or shaping it into usable forms, into engines and rails and machines. Technological changes in the textile industry encompassed the spinning jenny and the flying shuttle.

CHANGES IN THE LIVES OF WORKERS

A typical work situation before the Industrial Revolution could be found in a rural English village, where most of the people made their livings by farming, sometimes on their own acreage, often using common land for raising crops, sometimes tilling the vast acres owned by the lord of the manor. In addition, work like spinning and weaving was carried on in humble cottages. Weaving, blacksmithing, and cobbling were done in village workshops.

Every part of human endeavor was somehow affected by the ascendancy of the machine over nature in the Industrial Revolution.

As factories sprang up, masses of displaced farmers crowded into industrial cities. And as factories mass produced goods, they put the cottage worker and the village tradesperson and artisan out of work. And they, too, like the displaced farmer, went to industrial areas to compete for work. In 1770, the industrial city of Manchester, England, had a total population of 25,000 people. By 1850, the number had reached 350,000 people. Factory work came at a price. The worker lost independence, privacy, a vital contact with nature, and the ability to augment the food for his family with a small vegetable garden and the raising of a few animals. Now workers were bought and controlled by factory owners and capitalists who invested in the factory. A new aristocracy was built on the backs of labor.

The owners were free of regulations governing their treatment of workers in this " leave-alone" economy. Nothing prevented owners from crowding workers into filthy, rat-infested, crime-ridden slums without sources of water or proper means of disposing of waste. Sewage was let to run in the streets. Nothing prevented owners from hiring men, women, and children and paying them the poorest of salaries, or from forcing them to work 12 to 14 hours a day, six and sometimes seven days a week. Nothing forced them to prevent injuries and fatalities caused by large, powerful machines. Owners and city governments were not required to take responsibility for the sick and injured, for homeless children, the elderly, or the destitute. And these abominable practices were transplanted to the Brave New World, founded on the rights to life, liberty, and the pursuit of happiness.

Money-making crops replaced smaller, diverse gardens. Farmers, instead of growing a variety of vegetables to meet family and community needs, turned entirely to the raising of a single crop like cotton or wool to supply textile mills. Family-run farms were absorbed by what were called agri-businesses, sowing massive amounts of fruits and vegetables, to be sent to canneries and to feed markets all over the world. The actual work was performed by cheap labor that had no financial stake in the land and actually starved while being surrounded by foodstuffs. Cattle were eventually mass produced for the meat packing houses. Whole forests were cut to be processed in lumber mills. Other mass-produced products changed even the ways of constructing buildings and conducting trades.

Victorian Views of Work

Essentially, the abuse of the worker was buttressed by theology. Max Weber, a groundbreaking sociologist, argued that capitalistic society, from the Reformation until the early twentieth century, was shaped by religious doctrine: the hierarchical view of work and the conviction that the rich were rich because God loved them and that the poor deserved their poverty. Philosopher John Locke (1632–1704), who had tremendous influence on the formation of the United States constitution, adopted a view of work radically different from what Weber called the Protestant Ethic. Locke argued that all men, not just wealthy nobles, had certain natural rights. Among these was every individual's right to his own work. No person, he asserted, can call another person's labor his own.

By the middle of the eighteenth century, other economic philosophies were in the ascendancy, working hand-in-glove with the industrialists and the aristocracy. These philosophers, who came to prominence and influence with the rise of the Industrial Revolution, promulgated economic ideas that worked to the detriment and degradation of the laborer. From France in the eighteenth century came the philosophy of laissez-faire, or "leave things alone." According to this philosophical school, there was a natural economic order that should not be upset by government interference. Practically speaking, this resulted in unfettered capitalism. In Great Britain, laissez-faire was embraced and promulgated by Scottish economist Adam Smith. Smith's theories (published in 1776 in *Wealth of Nations*, a book that became the bible of economists), were eagerly adopted by the new wealthy merchants, manufacturers, bankers, and other businesspersons. For 250 years Smith's theories contributed to the misery of the common man.

The American System

In the middle of the nineteenth century, American industrialists developed a new method of manufacturing called the American System. This involved the making of small parts with the use of machines, which parts would then be put together by workers into a final product such as a firearm. Eventually, Henry Ford modified the idea to produce his notorious assembly line, which required workers to do one small repetitive task at machines that were set at a rapid, unrelenting pace. The oppressive, tyrannical assembly line, which led inevitably to an increase in workplace accidents, was adopted by every large industry in the United States.

Worker-Friendly Economic Philosophies

While laissez-faire and utilitarianism directed and dominated the workforce in the nineteenth century, reformers, sickened by the plight of laborers, presented radically different ideologies to improve the lives of workers. One of the most successful of these was socialism. Socialists insisted that, only with the abolition of free enterprise and laissez-faire, could society achieve social justice, freedom, and equality. Replacing private ownership with public ownership would give workers back their labor, giving workers joint ownership in the factories for which they labored, and closing the chasm between the haves and the have-nots. Socialism sprang up in France and moved to England and America, where converts to the philosophy—reformers like Robert Owen and others—believed that, by establishing socialistic communes as examples to the rest of the world, socialism would soon spread to become the predominant political structure of all nations.

In the mid nineteenth century, Frederick Engels, an Englishman, and Karl Marx, a German, developed a more radical wing of socialism sometimes called Marxism, sometimes communism. Marx believed that the value in any product resided in the labor that went into it, that workers had been alienated from the capitalistic societies they served, and that workers had been reduced to wage slavery in their struggle against the ruling class. Engels wrote: "Workers of the world unite! You have nothing to lose but your chains!"

THE NOVEL AND LABOR ISSUES

At the same time that the Industrial Revolution was taking place, a new literary genre was taking hold. This was the novel, which had its birth in England in the eighteenth century with such figures as Daniel Defoe, Henry Fielding, and Samuel Richardson. From its inception to the current day, the novel has been a genre of social commentary. The English writer Charles Dickens was its most enduring master. But other novelists of the time, though perhaps not as prolific or famous, were more courageous, forward-looking reformers: Mrs. Elizabeth Gaskell, Charles Kingsley, George Gissing, and Israel Zangwill.

In the United States, work problems emerged throughout the nineteenth century in the novels of Herman Melville, Harriet Beecher Stowe, George Washington Cable, Charlotte Perkins Gilman, Helen Hunt Jackson, Edward Bellamy, and William Dean Howells, among others. The flowering and proliferation of the social protest novel in the United States came in the early decades of the nineteenth century with the works of Upton Sinclair, Theodore Dreiser, Frank Norris, Ida Tarbell, Jack London, and others regarded as muckrakers.

The Works Chosen for This Volume

The literary works were chosen for this volume with regard to their consideration of a variety of labor issues in different decades of the nineteenth and twentieth centuries. The present inquiry ranges in time from a memoir published in 1831 to a novel published in 2001. The works considered offer pictures of a wide range of laborers: slaves in salt mines; domestic workers; workers in paper mills, iron mills, and stockyards; migrant farm workers; fast-food workers; hospital workers; telephone solicitors; steelworkers, and others.

The Plan

The volume is organized roughly into several chronological periods. It begins with five works in the nineteenth century, when the Industrial Revolution had begun to restructure Western civilization and determine the direction and character of work in the modern world. Two classic novels in the early twentieth century cover a time of exploitation and organized labor protest. An extensive series of interviews gives a broad range of portraits of human mechanization in the 1960s and 1970s during a time of rampant consumerism and social rebellion. The final selections, bringing the volume up to the twenty-first century, enlarge on the work of adolescents. The organization allows one to see a course of change in the workplace from the early days of the Industrial Revolution to the present day.

Each chapter is divided into three major sections: the historical context, the vision of labor in the work and the issues it raises, and applicable labor issues since the work's publication.

Work and Its Context

Mary Prince's 1831 *History of Mary Prince*, a memoir of her life as a slave, presents details of the actual work a slave woman performed in some of the most perilous and grueling of circumstances. This, the story of a person who does not own her own labor, is informed by the institution of slavery and the slave trade, with particular emphasis on work conditions in the West Indies and North America.

Charles Dickens's *Hard Times* (1854), a fitting introduction to the plight of the worker during the rise of the Industrial Revolution, appears against the early rise of factory towns, especially in the north of England, at a time of labor protest and parliamentary legislation that was both friendly and unfriendly to laborers.

"The Paradise of Bachelors and The Tartarus of Maids" (1855), by Herman Melville, contrasts the comfortable life in London's legal temples with a rural paper mill in New England. The detailed fictional picture of each stage of paper-making resonates with issues raised in reality in factories throughout New England, like the textile mills in Lowell, Massachusetts. Young farmwomen were drawn from farms into hazardous work places and poverty, from which situations the American labor movement emerged.

Rebecca Harding Davis's *Life in the Iron Mills* (1861) continues the story of rampant capitalism and the tyranny of the machine in the nation's burgeoning iron and steel mills, to which poor British and European immigrants were attracted and sacrificed.

Melville's *Bartleby, the Scrivener* (1853) is the only viable portrait of the daily routine, including its material particulars, in an office in New York's financial district. The cast of lawyers, brokers, and clerks on New York City's Wall Street is presented as the consequence of capitalism and the Industrial Revolution.

Upton Sinclair's *The Jungle* (1906) is a classic work that goes deeply into the demeaning and dehumanizing toil of stockyard workers and the details of their personal lives. The novel is presented in the framework of the rise and abuse of immigrant labor in the early years of the twentieth century, and the worker's hope that trade unions and socialism would relieve their misery.

In the background of John Steinbeck's 1939 novel, *The Grapes of Wrath*, a masterpiece about the daily lives of a migrant family, is the system that created the economic disaster called the Great Depression, with its callous wealthy owners of agribusinesses and its poverty stricken roving migrants.

The novel at midcentury was less concerned about workplace issues, but in 1972, new attention was turned to labor issues by Studs Terkel's *Working*, an extensive and highly praised series of interviews about labor in the 1960s and early 1970s. These interviews are played out in a culture of consumerism, discontent, and social upheaval: struggles for civil rights for women and African Americans, disruption over the nation's involvement in the Vietnam War, and outrage at the presidential scandal called Watergate.

The last chapter, on fiction intended for young adults, explores the effect of a parent's migratory work on his children (Zilpha Snyder's *The Velvet Room*, 1965), the work of a teenage waitress (Joan Bauer's *Hope Was Here*, 2000), and a wide variety of work done by teenagers (Anne

Mazer's *Working Days*, 1997). These stories are presented within a long and sordid history of children at work and the changing dynamic of work in the final decades of the twentieth century.

Workplace Issues

In varying degrees and situations, the same fundamental work issues, like low wages and long hours, arise in every decade, in every century. But several of the works presented here go beyond particular issues to generalize on the root causes of worker distress, to address the system behind the mistreatment and suffering of those whose labor sustains the very structure that destroys them. In *The History of Mary Prince*, slavery allows one person to legally own another person's body (and those of his or her children in perpetuity), including that person's labor. Other works—most notably *Hard Times*, *The Jungle*, and *The Grapes of Wrath*—expose an exploitative economic system that places capital and profit above the public's interest and above the worker's welfare. Writers see the tragedy in the supremacy and the tyranny of the fast-paced, relentless machine to which the humanity of the worker is sacrificed. They see the damage done by the growing chasm between owners and workers.

The root issues are consistently unemployment, poverty-level wages, and killing hours. Physical dangers and damage are equally threatening in the workplace. In these works, laborers are threatened, maimed, and killed in or by the workplace—by machines that mangle and slaughter, and by poisonous lint, chemicals, and metallic dust that inevitably destroy the workers' lungs and take their lives.

The works in this volume address a variety of other profoundly serious problems that have plagued workers for centuries: the refusal to provide them with compensation for injuries suffered on the job, the lack of job security, blacklisting, the hiring of children, the collusion of owners and law enforcement to suppress workers, and the abusive policies of company-run stores.

These are the complaints about practices that cause physical damage. They also result in psychological devastation, equally as painful and largely unacknowledged by owners, companies, managers, foremen, and government agencies. Other conditions are rarely addressed by regulators and reformers, though they cause as much psychological pain as accidents cause physical pain: humiliation by bosses and customers, the hopelessness that comes from dashed aspirations, the moral quandaries caused by being forced to lie and cheat the public as part of the job, the sexual harassment, and the inevitable escape into alcohol.

The one hopeful idea that surfaces in several of the earlier works, especially, is the possibility of a better life, a more humane society through reforms and supportive labor unions. In works after 1960, however, even in the multiple interviews conducted by Studs Terkel, this hope had largely disappeared from the conversation.

FURTHER READING

Burnett, John, ed. *Annals of Labour*. Bloomington: Indiana University Press, 1974.

Clayton, Robert and David Roberts. *A History of England 1688 to the Present*, Vol II. Englewood Cliffs, NJ: Prentice-Hall, Inc., 1980.

Foner, Philip. *A History of the Labor Movement in the United States*. 4 vols. New York: International Publishers, 1947–1964.

Halevy, Elie. *History of the English People in the Nineteenth Century*. London: Benn, 1950.

Hobsbawm, E. J. *Industry and Empire*. London: Penguin Books, 1968.

Pike, E. Royston. *Hard Times: Human Documents of the Industrial Revolution*. New York: Praeger, 1966.

Plumb, J. H. *England in the Eighteenth Century*. Aylesbury, UK: Hunt Barnard and Co., 1950.

Zinn, Howard. *A People's History of the United States*. New York: HarperCollins, 1980.

1

Mary Prince's *History of Mary Prince, a West Indian Slave*

The situation in which unprotected workers were turned into machines, laid out in Charles Dickens's *Hard Times*, was a direct result of the Industrial Revolution. An even more dehumanizing system of labor that flourished in the nineteenth century at the same time that the Industrial Revolution was transforming work in the Western World dates back to the beginnings of human history. This was the system of human slavery, by means of which the slaveholder owned the worker, body and soul, including, of course, the worker's labor. The descriptions of slave labor during the nineteenth century are preserved in more than 6,000 narratives written by slaves, some of which are referenced in the following study of work in Mary Prince's 1831 *History of Mary Prince, a West Indian Slave*. One of the classic slave narratives, Mary Prince's history was written after she gained her freedom in England and has the distinction of being the first slave narrative written by a woman. Her history has been chosen from the many extant slave narratives because of the specificity with which she deals with the actual work of a slave. In the last paragraph of her history she sums up her theme: she is trying to bring the plight of the slave to the attention of the British people:

> We don't mind hard work, if we had proper treatment, and proper wages like English servants, and proper time given in the week to keep us from breaking the Sabbath. But they won't give it: they will have work—work—work, night and day, sick or well, till we are quite done up. (Gates 215)

Broadly speaking, the work issues raised by Mary Prince are applicable to labor throughout the ages: long hours, multiple tasks, too little rest, little or no wages, hopelessness, the owner's unreasonable expectations, workplace threats to life and health, and sexual abuse. Still, the situation of literal slaves differed in kind from that of industrial laborers, who were often described as factory slaves. First, slaves were literally owned; they were sold at auction like animals and bred like animals. Second, the children and grandchildren of slaves were automatically the property of the parents' owners in perpetuity. Third, as the literal property of their masters, slaves were usually forbidden from learning to read, from marrying, and from participating in religious services. Fourth, families of slaves were not recognized or treated as families. Members of a family could be and were sold to separate owners, separating even small children from their mothers. Fifth, whereas white female workers were often sexually abused by factory owners and managers, black women were routinely raped by owners for their own pleasure and to breed more slaves to work or to sell. Finally, unlike the white factory worker, black slaves were usually beaten brutally by savage owners.

THE SEQUENCE OF EVENTS IN MARY'S HISTORY

Mary's *History* was published after a lifetime of slave labor in the West Indies, after she gained her freedom in England, to which one of her masters had taken her from Antigua for a temporary stay. Because Mary Prince had limited writing skills, she had to dictate her story to a woman visiting the couple, the Pringles, who had taken Mary in. Thomas Pringle edited and published Mary's story, insisting in the introduction that Mary's own words had been retained. The immediate motive behind the publication was Mary's struggle to return to Antigua from England as a free woman, and her master's insistence that, although she was legally free as long as she remained in England, she would again be his slave if she returned to Antigua where he could and would assert his right of ownership. In pressing his own case, her former master maliciously maligned both Mary and her husband.

Mary was born in the West Indies, where British colonists enslaved black people like Mary and her mother and father. The episodes in her life are organized according to the various people who owned her, and consist chiefly of information about the work she was required to do and the punishments she suffered for failing to perform her work to the satisfaction of her owners.

At the time of her birth, Mary and her mother belonged to Charles Myners and her father to a Mr. Trimmingham. When Myners died, she and her mother were sold to a Captain Darrel who then gave them to the Williams family. Mary became the property of the Williams' young daughter Betsy. Here her mother had a favored position as a household slave. Those who worked in the fields did the most grueling work and were regarded as being on the lowest rung of slave society. Although Miss Betsy called Mary "my little nigger," Mary regarded this as "the happiest period" of her life (187). Even at this young age, however, she had to perform light chores.

At the age of 12 years, she was "hired out" (188) by Mrs. Williams to a Mrs. Pruden, in a forced separation from her mother and siblings. In her new home, she was responsible for taking care of a new baby and being a companion for two older children, one of whom shared all her lessons with Mary.

Another change in position came when her owner, Mrs. Williams, died and Mary learned that she and two of her sisters would be sold by Mr. Williams to pay for his wedding to another woman, even though Mary was actually the property of Williams' daughter, Betsy. It meant Mary's separation from her family. The day came when Mary and her sisters were led by their mother to the slave auction and eventually sold to different owners.

She began a new life in the household of a "Captain I___" (192) whose name she and Pringle were reluctant to provide because stories of his cruelty might hurt his children who could be innocent of their father's crimes. Here she observed the sadistic treatment of other slaves before physical violence came to be directed against her. Mary remained with Captain and Mrs. I___ for more than five years. She was driven to run home to her mother at one point but was returned to her master who whipped her almost every day.

Her next episode was a four-week voyage to Turks Island, some 200 miles northeast of Bermuda. She was placed aboard a sloop without being able to say goodbye to her mother, father, or siblings. On board ship, with provisions running low, she was kept alive by her fellow slaves who shared with her the food they had brought for the voyage.

Upon her arrival at Grand Quay, she found that she had been sold to a Mr. D____. Here she was put to work in salt ponds on his property. Mr. D____ was as vicious as Captain and Mrs. I____, and the work in the salt ponds far harder and more damaging than any work she had done before. Here she remained for 10 years, seeing her now deranged mother only once in all this time.

When Mr. D____ returned to Bermuda proper in his retirement, he took Mary with him. She was required to do both field and housework, which was still less arduous than the salt ponds. But Mr. D____ had not had a change of character with his return to the center of Bermuda society and continued beating his slaves and daughters. Moreover, he developed what Mary called indecent habits.

At the age of 28 she came under the control of John Wood, who took her with him to Antigua and eventually bought her for about 67 pounds. The physical ailments she suffered as a result of her work in the salt ponds grew worse and worse during her long stay with the Woods, among the cruelest of her owners. During this period, she was introduced to religion for the first time and became an active participant in the Moravian Church. In 1826 in the Moravian Church, she married Daniel James, a black man who had been able to buy his freedom. They were not allowed to marry in the Church of England, which outlawed marriages between slaves and freemen. She was lashed and constantly berated by the Woods for marrying Daniel.

The Woods refused all her offers to buy her own freedom, and they took her with them on a trip to England to put their son in school there. Here she became too ill to do the heavy work demanded of her.

Legally, Mary was free as long as she was in England; however, she knew no one to whom she could turn and so was terrified when the Woods threw her out on several occasions. After 13 years as the Woods' slave and a few months after having arrived in England, Mary left their home for good. She found her way to a Moravian Church whose congregation allowed her to stay. Shortly she moved in with a poor black couple who took care of her. She learned of the Anti-Slavery Society and the Quaker Fellowship that pled her case before the courts and then to Mr. Wood to allow her to return to her husband in Antigua as a free woman. But the courts could not help her, and Wood continued to deny her her freedom.

Eventually, after several part-time jobs, she found a more permanent position with Mr. and Mrs. Pringle, who treated her well, taught her, encouraged her church participation, pled the case for her freedom in Antigua, and edited and published her history.

A supplement, appended to Mary's history, written by Thomas Pringle, illustrated Mr. Wood's attempt to smear Mary's character while refusing her freedom. Pringle offered several testimonies that contradicted Woods' statements, and concluded with references to other slaves in his antislavery argument.

THE HISTORICAL CONTEXT

Slavery is the system in which human beings are owned as property, chiefly for the purpose of securing their labor. It is a practice as old as human history and has appeared in almost every culture—in early nomadic societies, in fourth-millennium Sumeria, in eighteenth-century B.C. Babylonia, in second-millennium Egypt, in sixth century B.C. India, in sixth century B.C. Persia, and in 1200 B.C. Greece, to name a few. Slavery was instituted in the New World wherever European colonizers landed, and it continued as a lawful institution in the Americas until after the American Civil War.

In the fifteenth century, the Spanish and Portuguese made slaves of Native Americans in the New World. But soon they replaced most of these slaves with blacks they either bought from traders in Africa or hunted down themselves. English colonists, who often raided Spanish and Portuguese ships for slaves, put them to work chiefly in sugar and coffee plantations in the New World's southern hemisphere. In the northern hemisphere, particularly the southern United States, they were forced to work on tobacco, rice, sugar cane, and cotton plantations.

Mary Prince's slave narrative takes place in the English West Indian colony of Bermuda, consisting of a chain of 300 small Islands, 20 of which are inhabited. British colonists landed there in 1609, and it was officially made a British colony in 1684. Some 15 million slaves were brought to the Americas, including Bermuda, from the sixteenth through the nineteenth centuries. As in the American south, so in Bermuda: The economy rested on and revolved around the ownership of slave labor. A triangle, based on the slave trade, was at the center of the New World economy: The English headed from English ports to the west coast of Africa, their ships loaded with English goods. In Africa, they traded their goods for African slaves and then, in what was called the Middle Passage, headed for the West Indies. Only 80 percent of the slaves survived. The West Indies was the major market for African slaves in the New World, in part because it was closest to Africa and there was less likelihood of further deaths. Most of the slaves in North America came from the West Indies rather than directly from Africa. In the West Indies, the end of the second leg of the triangle, the English merchants exchanged slaves for the West Indies' natural resources, chiefly sugar. Mary Prince also mentions loading British ships with salt. In the seventeenth and eighteenth centuries, the British ships, upon leaving the West Indies, often stopped in New England to sell sugar and molasses needed for the manufacture of rum.

By 1816, the land had been so depleted in Bermuda's islands that agricultural products, like cotton, had virtually dried up, and by 1829, the only viable export was salt, the industry in which Mary Prince was forced to work. Six of the islands contained salt ponds; Turks Island, where Mary worked, was one of the largest.

Britain outlawed the slave trade in 1807 and outlawed slavery itself in 1833, two years after Mary Prince published her history. Quakers, who helped Mary survive in England, had been active in the struggle against slavery since 1724. In the United States, slavery officially came to an end with the Thirteenth Amendment to the Constitution in 1865.

SLAVE WORK

Most of the work of slaves was conducted on plantations where sugar, tobacco, and cotton were grown. Slave narratives tended to focus on the behavior of their masters, punishments, personal relationships, and the struggle for freedom. Detailed descriptions of the actual work they did are given less frequently. But several sources do provide graphic pictures of various kinds of labor. One of the most valuable pictures of work on a plantation came from the pen of a northern engineer, Frederick Law Olmsted in his *A Journey in the Back Country*. Olmsted described slaves arriving to work in the fields before sunrise and working until after dark. Plowing with mules in the fields was usually the work of girls. They managed double teams of mules pulling heavy plows. A slave with a snapping whip followed the plow girls to keep them working at a brisk pace. Another category of field hands was composed of teams or gangs who did the hoeing. Olmsted watched 200 slaves moving ploddingly across the field in parallel lines. A slave with a whip also walked behind these men. The picking of the cotton crop, which had to be done thoroughly at top speed, was also part of the back-breaking work of field hands (Olmsted 70–93).

Solomon Northrup, a slave for 12 years on a cotton plantation, augments Olmsted's account of the work performed there. Each slave was given a sack to drag behind him or her and fill with cotton, which was then dumped into a basket at the end of the row. The overseer expected each worker to pick 200 pounds of cotton a day. Anyone who fell short of the 200 pounds was beaten. After the weighing, there were further chores: feeding mules and swine, cutting wood, grinding corn for the last meal of the day—around midnight—and for the meal the following day. Slaves, who slept on boards with sticks of wood for pillows, lived in terror of oversleeping and being punished. After the cotton was picked, slaves were responsible for making the 400-pound bales of cotton and for getting them to market (Northrup 163–75).

Basil Hall, a captain in the British navy, described his visit to a rice plantation in 1827 and1828. One of the jobs of the slaves was to build dams to regulate water in the fields where rice was to be grown. Hall described slaves working in a long line, like a row of ants, and carrying baskets of dirt on their heads. He noted that this was hard, heavy labor that left the weaker slaves and women looking exhausted in the afternoon. Slaves prepared the soil for planting, sowed the rice seeds, and reaped the crops. They made long trenches for cultivation of rice and placed each seed carefully by hand. Afterward, the fields were alternately flooded, drained of water, dried out, and flooded again. The constant necessity to stand in water for long periods of time, the heat, and diseases carried by mosquitoes attracted to the water resulted in one of the highest mortality rates of any field work. As Hall writes in a chapter of Rose's *A Documentary History of Slavery in North America*:

> The cultivation of rice was described to me as by far the most unhealthy work in which the slaves were employed; and, in spite of every care, that they sank under it in great numbers. The causes of this dreadful mortality, are the constant moisture and heat of the atmosphere, together with the alternate floodings and dryings of the fields, on which the negroes are perpetually at work, often ankle-deep in mud, with their bare heads exposed to the fierce rays of the sun. At such seasons every white man leaves the spot, as a matter of course. (Rose 304)

Work in the salt ponds was equally damaging. Most of the ponds, contrary to the picture Mary gave, were public property and the work seasonal. Anyone who had the slaves to work in the ponds had access to them. Workers stood in the salt ponds and shoveled salt into buckets or onto wooden rafts. They were then required to push heavy wheelbarrows of the salt through the sand to a central place where the salt was emptied and covered with palmetto fronds.

MARY'S WORK AS A SLAVE

In the work history of Mary Prince, one finds issues that have plagued workers throughout the past and to the present day—for example, the hours demanded of a laborer. But in a situation in which persons do not own their own labor, these workplace problems became amplified. In her young childhood, Mary and her family had the less arduous jobs in the range of slave labor. Mary's mother worked as a household slave; her father worked for a ship builder; young Mary herself was a companion to—in other words, the pet of—a young girl in the family; and all the younger slave children were given light chores. At 12 years of age she was hired out to a neighboring woman who only required her to take care of the baby of the house.

Before she was in her teens, she was sold to a harsh, cruel couple. Her work as a children's nurse was the same, but the manner in which she was treated made her work a nightmare. Part of her unhappiness came from observing the work demanded of a slave named Hetty and the abuse Hetty suffered at the hands of her owners. Hetty was required to milk the cows, prepare the meals, and, at the end of the day, herd the flock of sheep home and pen them up, drive the herd of cattle home and tie them up, feed and rub down the horse, feed the pigs, turn down the beds at the end of the day, dress the children for bed, and put them to bed. On the night of Mary's arrival in the household, Hetty had not completed one of her chores by bedtime and was savagely beaten by her master.

Mary, scarcely in her teens, initially had a heavy workload on the plantation. She was responsible for washing and baking, preparing raw cotton and wool, and washing the floors, in addition to child care. She was routinely kept awake most of the night, taking the directions of her mistress to do miscellaneous chores. When Hetty died, Mary inherited Hetty's chores on top of her own. She had to milk 11 cows before sunrise. She had to care for the cattle, and take on additional household duties and additional child care duties.

Eventually, Mary was introduced to some of the most difficult labor a slave in Bermuda could do: work in the salt ponds of Turks Island. There she and the other slaves shoveled salt from the pond into buckets. They worked from four A.M. until sundown, and at times, throughout the night, with two short breaks to eat boiled cornmeal. The primary job required them to stand in salt water up to their knees throughout the day. At the end of the day, they shoveled the salt they had gathered into wheelbarrows and pushed these heavy loads through sand to a central point where the salt was mounded into hills. After this, they went to the sea to try to get the encrusted salt off their bodies and their tools.

At times, when ships came into harbor to take on salt, Mary and the other slaves worked throughout the night, measuring salt to load onto the ships. They also had hard work to do throughout the night when additional sea water was needed in the salt ponds. It was their job to painstakingly turn a heavy machine to pump the water from the sea into the ponds. Mary also described going into the harbor in small boats and diving from the boats to the bottom of the sea to bring up large stones to build walls. On Sundays they were required to wash the bags they used to haul salt.

After 10 years of this work on Turks Island, Mary's owner took her to Bermuda proper. She describes her jobs there as heavy but not nearly as hurtful as working in the salt ponds. In Bermuda she was responsible for all the household work, miscellaneous errands, and the upkeep of the cows and horses. She was also "rented out," by the man who owned her labor to do other people's washing.

She was after a short time sold to John Wood and taken to Antigua. In the Wood household she was responsible for the children, but her primary job was the washing each week of two massive bundles of clothes in a stream. The bundles were so heavy they had to be lifted by two people. She was able to make a little money of her own, when her master and mistress were out of town, by taking in other peoples' washing and buying and selling small provisions.

When she went with the family to their country quarters, she got a glimpse of the lives of field hands who, she observed, were worked very hard and inadequately fed. Their work was not over even after returning from the fields because they had to then feed the cattle. The only day they had to sell provisions they'd gathered was on Sunday. They had no day of rest.

Mary accompanied her owners on a trip to England under the mistaken impression that her physical ailments, acquired in the salt ponds, would be cured. However, the opposite was true. Her health worsened; therefore her work became almost impossible to do. Her job, as in Antigua, was to wash immense bundles of clothes by kneeling or sitting on the floor before the tub in the wash house. When her owners moved to larger quarters in London, Mary and the cook were charged with washing five large bags of clothing, which Mary was physically unable to do. A crisis occurred when the two months' "great washing" was scheduled. This included heavy items like large bed coverlets and bed ticks—bed-sized bags, stuffed with various materials to be used as mattresses. At this point, Mary used her master's threat to throw her out of the house to leave forever.

THE BRUTAL OWNER

In slavery the persistent workplace problems of a cruel boss, sexual abuse, and injurious working conditions were writ large. The merciless boss or owner has been and continues, to a lesser extent, to be a workplace problem. But when the worker's labor is legally owned by the boss, there is little or no check on the owner's behavior. In some instances, the owner's realization that the slaves were very valuable cash commodities restrained them from killing slaves or from rendering them incapable of working. But more often, as Mary Prince described it, the master or mistress had little compunction about torturing or maiming workers or even slowly killing them.

Several cases of owners torturing their workers stuck in Mary's mind. Hetty, who was almost worked to death and was routinely beaten, was finally beaten to death during her pregnancy. Daniel, an elderly cripple at the salt ponds, was constantly beaten and had salt poured into his wounds, preventing the wounds from ever healing. Ben, another salt pond worker, was strung up and beaten throughout the day and then had a bayonet driven through his foot. Sarah, an old woman, was beaten severely because she could not push her wheelbarrow through the sand fast enough. Then she was picked up and thrown into a bush of thorns. These puncture wounds caused multiple infections, from which she died.

Mary herself was repeatedly strung up by her wrists, and piteously lashed by her last three owners. She was beaten with ropes, cart whips, or cowhides. One of her mistresses also hit her repeatedly on her face and head with her fists. Moira Ferguson, in her introduction to one of the editions of Prince's history, suggests that these constant head blows could well have caused Mary's early blindness. For the five years she was owned by Captain I___, she was beaten almost every day.

THE EFFECT OF WORK ON LIFE AND HEALTH

Arguably, the greatest threats to the slave's life and limb were the floggings they received when their work was not to the boss's satisfaction—when they accidentally broke a pitcher, when an animal they were responsible for got loose, when they moved too slowly, or when they did not pick the required amount of cotton or other produce, for instance. The infections in the open sores produced by the lash were often fatal.

Even the health and lives of domestic servants, who had easier lives than field hands, were constantly placed in jeopardy through overwork.

One example in Mary Prince's life as both domestic and hard laborer was the overwork and sleep deprivation that not only injured the slaves' health but left them subject to accidents and delays in work. For this they were beaten. Of the salt ponds, she wrote:

> If we could not keep up with the rest of the gang of slaves, we were put in the stocks, and severely flogged the next morning. Yet, not the less, our master expected, after we had thus been kept from our rest, and our limbs rendered stiff and sore with ill usage, that we should still go through the ordinary tasks of the day all the same. (Gates 199)

As a result of standing up to their knees in salt water for 15 hours a day, she and other slaves developed salt boils on their legs—boils that often went all the way to the bone:

> I was given a half barrel and a shovel, and had to stand up to my knees in water, from four o'clock in the morning till nine, when we were given some Indian corn boiled in water, which we were obliged to swallow as fast as we could for fear the rain should come on and melt the salt. We were then called again to our tasks, and worked through the heat of the day; the sun flaming upon our heads like fire, and raising slat blisters in those parts which were not completely covered. Our feet and legs, from standing in the salt water for so many hours, soon became full of dreadful boils, which eat down in some cases to the very bone, afflicting the sufferers with great torment. (Gates 198)

As they pushed heavy wheelbarrows, sand was ground into the salt sores on their feet, and as they dived for large stones, they were in danger of drowning.

Although Mary did not seem to make the connection, it is obvious that her 10 years' work in the salt pond left her with what she called rheumatism but was likely a severe form of arthritis. Within a year of leaving the salt works, she became crippled. Her work on Turks Island destroyed her health, leaving her a virtual invalid, often bedridden, in constant pain, with swollen, stiff, arthritic joints. At times she was incapable of moving her legs.

Her physical ailments were worsened by her new assignment of washing heavy loads of her owners' clothes in a cold pond.

SEXUAL ABUSE OF SLAVES

Sexual abuse of workers, seen frequently even in the twenty-first century, when a boss holds a woman's job hostage in exchange for sexual favors, was common to slavery. As Moira Ferguson points out, Mary seemed reluctant to speak of sexual abuse directly, as her American counterparts did. Still, the clues are there. Seemingly, the first experience Mary had of this came when she was taken to be sold at auction:

> At length the vendue master, who was to offer us for sale like sheep or cattle, arrived, and asked my mother which was the eldest. She said nothing, but pointed to me. He took me by the hand, and led me out into the middle of the street, and turning me slowly round, exposed me to the view of those who attended the vendue. I was soon surrounded by strange men, who examined and handled me in the same manner that a butcher would a calf or lamb he was about to purchase, and who talked about my shape and size in like words. (Gates 191)

It is also hard to escape the notion that beatings were a form of sexual sadism. Girls and women as well as boys and men were stripped naked to be strung up and lashed. At the house of Captain D.___, two small boys were whipped daily for no reason whatsoever. Mary's comment is suggestive: "Both my master and my mistress seemed to think that they had a right to ill-use them at their pleasure." (194) On Turks Island as well, Mr. D.___ "has often striped me naked, hung me up by the wrists, and beat me with the cow skin, with his own hand, till my body was raw with gashes." (199)

Mary also made reference to the indecency of Mr. D.____, who brought her to Bermuda after 10 years on Turks Island. Even though the position she found herself in after leaving Mr. D.___ was more demanding and cruel, she preferred it to her work for an "indecent" boss:

> He had an ugly fashion of stripping himself quite naked, and ordering me then to wash him in a tub of water. This was worse to me than all the licks. Sometimes when he called me to wash him I would not come, my eyes were so full of shame. He would then come to beat me. . . . I then told him I would not live longer with him, for he was a very indecent man—very spiteful, and too indecent; with no shame for his servants, no shame for his own flesh. (202, 203)

Mary Prince made only a passing reference to other abuses (as when, in a footnote, her editor spoke of the several children that her enslaved sister had borne by the man who owned her). But it was common throughout the history of slavery for masters to misuse slave women sexually and to father children to increase the ranks of the slave population. Nineteenth-century American slaves, both men and women, were more likely to attest to this practice, than were British-held slaves. Frederick Douglass, an ex-slave who became one of the most prominent leaders of the nineteenth century, was told secretly that his real father was his white master. Douglass also observed the many slave women taken as mistresses by their owners and the large brood of mulatto children on most plantations, children who were kept enslaved by their fathers. The situation became harder to deny as the complexion of slaves became lighter and lighter.

Harriet Jacobs, author of another well-known slave narrative, also wrote of instances in which her master, Dr. Flint, fathered children by his slaves. Harriet described how, when she was in her early teens, Flint began stalking her:

> But I now entered my fifteenth year—a sad epoch in the life of a slave girl. My master began to whisper foul words in my ear.... He tried his utmost to corrupt the pure principles my grandmother had instilled. He peopled my young mind with unclean images, such as only a vile monster could think of. I turned from him with disgust and hatred.
>
> . . .
>
> Even the little child, who is accustomed to wait on her mistress and her children, will learn before she is twelve years old, why it is that her mistress hates such and such a one among the slaves.... She will become prematurely knowing in evil things. Soon she will learn to tremble when she hears her master's footfall. (Harriet Jacobs, quoted in Gates 361).

When her master threatened to force her to go with him on an extended out-of-town trip and force her to live in a cottage he was building for her, Harriet managed to hide from him in a cramped storage space over a white woman's bedroom. Here, before she made her way to freedom, she lived for seven years while her master searched for her relentlessly and punished her friends and family.

THE RECONFIGURATION OF WORK
IN THE 1880s

Even after slavery was officially outlawed in the American South, a system of work arose in the aftermath of the Civil War that was in many ways as brutal as slavery. Thousands and thousands of black people and thousands of farm and plantation owners now saw the collapse of a system in which one group thrived economically by the labor they owned in the persons of slaves.

After the war, however, businessmen and owners of large farms in the South were forced to accept that they could no longer lawfully own other human beings, body and soul. However, they were able to develop a new exploitative economic system whereby they could still secure the labor of former slaves. This was accomplished in two ways. First, they offered to enter into work contracts with confused newly freed slaves who were wandering aimlessly about seeking ways to support themselves and their families. These contracts, in effect, bound black men, as well as poor whites, to their bosses for many years. The workers rarely received actual pay but were typically given script to spend at the company store. When the "pay" soon proved to be inadequate to survive on, they were forced to go into debt to their bosses, leading to the situation described in the popular song, in which they owed their souls to the company store. Any man who tried to leave was hunted down like a slave and was sentenced to prison.

The second way in which the businessman introduced the black man to the economy of the New South was by creating as many convicts as possible. Black men were arrested on the flimsiest of charges, chiefly idleness, and sentenced to long terms in prison, creating a new pool of labor that the rising businesses of the South could exploit. These free blacks were put to work, not only on large farms, but in newly established factories and on railroads. Naturally, employees were not required to pay the convicts they used, for the state owned the labor of its convicts.

In both the contract and convict situations, the black man, though technically free, still did not own his own labor.

The workplace situation of the former slaves and children of slaves was also changed by what has been called one of the significant diasporas, or dispersing of black people: a massive movement of African Americans from the South to the great cities of the North, among them, New York City, Washington, DC, Chicago, and Detroit. Although conditions in the North were more congenial than they had been in the South, in the

North as well as the South, African Americans were usually barred from all but the lowliest jobs. Advertisements for jobs were often listed under "whites only." Up to the mid-twentieth century, most African American women were still restricted to domestic positions and men to hard labor. They were expressly barred in the south from supervisory positions and from jobs as fire fighters, police officers, and bus drivers.

Even before the Civil War, white immigrants regarded free blacks as hateful competition for jobs in the North. In the Draft Riots of New York City during the Civil War, for instance, Irish immigrants swarmed over the city shooting, hanging, and setting fire to black workers. Frederick Douglass's remarks in 1853 were still true in the early decades of the twentieth century:

> The old avocations, by which colored men obtained a livelihood, are rapidly, unceasingly and inevitably passing into other hands; every hour sees the black man elbowed out of employment by some newly arrived emigrant.... Employments and calling, formerly monopolized by us, are so no longer.
>
> White men are becoming house-servants, cooks and stewards on vessels—at hotels.—They are porters, stevedores, wood-sawyers, hod-carriers, brick-makers, white-washers and barbers, so that the blacks can scarcely find the means of subsistence. (Fried 64)

As waves of immigrants poured into the United States in the late nineteenth and early twentieth centuries, the competition for jobs became even fiercer, dividing the labor force along racial lines rather than uniting it.

At the same time, labor was struggling for the right to organize and negotiate for better working conditions. Yet routinely, African Americans were barred from unions. In 1918, sociologist and historian W.E.B. Du Bois wrote in *The Crisis* that "in the present union movement, as represented by the American Federation of Labor, there is absolutely no hope of justice for an American of Negro descent" (Quoted in Fried 196).

In the last half of the twentieth century, African Americans held the greatest number of unskilled jobs; yet automation was severely decreasing demands for unskilled workers, and African Americans, up until the passage of the Civil Rights Act, found that barriers to apprenticeships, formal education, and training were continually thrown up to keep them in the ranks of the unskilled. But in the Civil Rights Act of 1964 Congress legislated the lifting of unnecessary barriers to employment, barriers based on racial discrimination. These included artificial barriers of required tests and qualifications that had no bearing on the work to be performed. Thus, a person whose job it was to load trucks should not be required to have a high school degree or be able to do advanced mathematics. This opened the way for both male and female African Americans to complain legally when there was evidence that companies were discriminately against them because of their race.

SLAVERY IN THE TWENTY-FIRST CENTURY

Even though slavery was found to be illegal in the American South in the 1860s, various forms of slavery have persisted in many parts of the world ever since, and they continue even into the twenty-first century. Slavery is a condition in which a slaveholder forces labor on a vulnerable worker with no protections: The worker can be worked more than 20 hours a day, for seven days a week, 365 days a year; there are no holidays or sick leave; no health and safety protections; and the pay is often nothing more than crude bed and board. Often the worker is bought and sold. Traditional slavery can be defined as the kind of slavery in which a person literally owns his laborers. Traditional slavery exists to this day in Mauritania, Niger, and Sudan. Women and children in particular are captured by government forces and sold.

But, as one learns in studying the postbellum American South, there are other forms of slavery. Another form of labor classified as slavery is called bonded labor, whereby hard labor or sex work is used to pay for loans, usually bearing astronomical interest. Workers have no choice but to enslave themselves to their bosses to whom they owe money they can never repay. Bonded labor, at one time found mainly in India, Pakistan, and Nepal, has spread throughout the world. In the twenty-first century it includes the practice of buying or kidnapping children in Asia and Africa. Despite laws prohibiting such practices, women, kidnapped or coerced in India, Asia, and Eastern Europe, are sent as sex slaves to all parts of the world, including Western Europe and North America. At the turn of the twenty-first century, for example, an Indian businessman in Berkeley, California, was tried and sentenced for trafficking in sex slaves, whom he brought from India to the United States.

The most despicable slavery, still very much alive in the twenty-first century is child slavery. In South Asia, West and Central Africa, and China, among other places, impoverished parents sell their children into slavery. Children, especially young girls, are also often kidnapped. Child slaves are expected to perform the lowliest work available, particularly as sex slaves. They are also used for such perilous work as drug trafficking, fireworks manufacturing, stone quarrying, and soldiering. Among the first social dangers to appear on the scene after the devastating earthquakes and tsunamis in Southeast Asia in early 2005 were crews of men looking there for orphaned children who could be kidnapped and enslaved.

Another form of labor, continuing especially in the twenty-first century in Burma, China, and Sudan, is forced work on public projects like road, bridge, railroad, and dam building or military service. In the case of forced labor, the enslaver is generally a government, and the slaves have been captured as war booty or political prisoners, or are convicts and even migrant workers.

In parts of Asia and Africa, many women become slaves when they marry, some at ages as young as 10 years. The three cases in which women have no choice in what happens to them are child marriage, forced marriage, and servile marriage. In these three cases, when women marry, they become domestic and sex slaves, often serving at the pleasure of first wives and usually becoming the objects of physical violence.

The United Nations and other global organizations have estimated that there are more than 27 million people living in slavery throughout the world in the twenty-first century. This is a higher number of enslaved human beings than at any time in history.

So in Mary Prince's history, many workplace issues that were writ large in slavery—especially overwork; industrial and agricultural dangers; harassment, including sexual harassment, by bosses—persist into the twenty-first century.

QUESTIONS AND PROJECTS

1. Compare and contrast the work performed by the maids in Melville's "Tartarus of Maids" with the work done by Mary Prince in the salt ponds.
2. Investigate and write about some pro-slavery arguments. What is the foundation of these arguments? Is the bottom line economic? Examine the language of one of these arguments. Does the language, the choice of words, suggest that slaves are regarded as things rather than human beings?
3. Write an essay on one of the three following topics: (a) the fundamental reasons why slave holders objected to their slaves learning to read (b) why they objected to slaves attending religious services; or (c) why in most areas, marriage between slaves was illegal.

4. Do research on details of the Middle Passage and make a report to the class.
5. Check the appendix to the third edition of Mary Prince's history. How does this contribute to the veracity of her history?
6. Do a newspaper search of the threat to orphans of the tsunami. Write a thoroughgoing report of the situation.
7. Obtain information from the EEOC regarding cases of sexual harassment submitted to the federal office. Write about the range of behavior that is reported.

FURTHER READING

Andrews, William L. *Black Women's Slave Narratives*. New York: Oxford University Press, 1987.

Baxter, Ralph H. *Sexual Harassment in the Work Place*. New York: Executive Enterprises Publications Co., 1981.

Burns, Alan. *History of the British West Indies*. London: George Allen and Unwin, 1954.

Clarke, Elissa. *Stopping Sexual Harassment*. Detroit: Labor Education and Research Project, 1980

Craton, Michael. *Sinews of Empire: A Short History of British Slavery*. New York: Anchor Books, 1974.

Ferguson, Moira, ed. *The History of Mary Prince*. Ann Arbor, MI: University of Michigan Press, 1987.

Fogel, Robert William and Stanley L. Engerman. *Time on the Cross: The Economics of American Negro Slavery*. 2 vols. Boston: Little, Brown, 1974.

Foster, Frances Smith. *Witnessing Slavery: The Development of Ante-Bellum Slave Narratives*. Westport, CT: Greenwood Press, 1979.

Fried, Albert. *Except to Walk Free: Documents and Notes in the History of American Labor*. New York: Anchor Books, 1974.

Gates, Henry Louis, Jr. *The Classic Slave Narratives*. New York: Penguin Books, 1987.

Hart, Richard. *Slaves Who Abolished Slavery*. Jamaica: University of the West Indies, 1980.

Higman, B. W. *Slave Populations of the British Caribbean 1807–1834*. Baltimore, MD: The Johns Hopkins University Press, 1984.

Northrup, Solomon. *Twelve Years a Slave*. Auburn, NY: Derby and Miller, 1853.

Olmsted, Frederick Law. *A Journey in the Back Country*. New York: Mason Bros., 1860.

Packwood, Cyril Outerbridge. *Chained on the Rock: Slavery in Bermuda*. New York: Baxter's Limited, 1975.

Ragan, Sandra L. *The Lynching of Language: Gender, Politics and Power in the Hill–Thomas Hearings*. Urbana, IL: University of Illinois Press, 1996.

Rose, Willie Lee, ed. *A Documentary History of Slavery in North America*. New York: Oxford University Press, 1976.

Smith, James E. *Slavery in Bermuda*. New York: Vantage Press, 1976.

Smitherman, Geneva, ed. *African American Women Speak Out on Anita Hill–Clarence Thomas*. Detroit: Wayne State University Press, 1995.

Stepto, Robert B. *From Behind the Veil: A Study of Afro-American Narrative*. Urbana, IL: University of Illinois Press, 1979.

Wesley, Charles H. *Negro Labor in the United States*. New York: Vanguard Press, 1931.

2

Charles Dickens's *Hard Times*

Charles Dickens's novel set in an industrial city in mid-nineteenth-century England is an early portrait of the fruits of the Industrial Revolution. Dickens addresses specific working-class problems in *Hard Times:* the deadening and polluted factory environment, the struggle to establish unions, and the owners' attitudes and unrestricted pursuit of capital that lead them to suppress all union protests and to blacklist any worker they suspect of being disloyal. Other issues, mentioned briefly, are the Poor Laws, the workhouses, and industrial accidents. One way in which inequality and injustice is demonstrated is in the unequal application of laws, in this case, divorce laws and criminal laws. But his main point is the spiritual starvation, inhumanity, and divisiveness produced by the ideas spawned in the ascendancy of the Almighty Machine.

PLOTS AND SUBPLOTS

Dickens's story about the convergence of members from three social groups in an industrial town called Coketown is divided into three parts or books: "Sowing," "Reaping," and "Garnering." "Book One: Sowing" concentrates on the seeds, meaning the ideologies, that support and are supported by the Industrial Revolution, and are sown in the community through schools and education and the endless recitals by those in power. In "Book Two: Reaping," disasters occur as a logical culmination of these ideas: the dissolution of Louisa's marriage, Tom's gambling and thievery, and the death of Stephen Blackpool. In "Book Three: Garnering," the characters who remain, especially Gradgrind, sorrowfully process what they have sown and reaped.

All the major groups and most of the characters are introduced in the first book. One group includes the privileged owners and gentry: Josiah Bounderby, the self-proclaimed self-made man who owns the bank and has a major interest in the local mills; Thomas Gradgrind, the local squire, mill owner, and a member of parliament; his wife; his son Tom (who goes to work for Bounderby) and his eldest daughter, Louisa. Also in the upper class group is Mrs. Sparsit, a high-born woman now reduced to waiting on Bounderby; and (introduced later) an opportunistic young man, Mr. James Harthouse, who is trying to learn the means of success from Bounderby.

A second group, who interact with the wealthy members of the community, are from the working class, chiefly mill worker Stephen Blackpool, his drunken wife, and Rachel, also a mill worker and the love of his life. In this group as well are Bitzer, a young man who plans to work his way up in the bank as Bounderby had done, a union organizer named Slackbridge, and an old woman named Pegler from a nearby village who comes to town periodically to gaze on Bounderby's mansion.

A third group is made up of the classless circus performers: Mr. Sleary, the circus owner, and Sissy Jupe, the abandoned daughter of one of the horse-riders in the circus.

In the beginning, the walls separating the three groups are high and thick. But as the action proceeds, fissures in the walls appear, revealing just how intricately the lives of those in the three groups are bound together.

The main, interlinking plots are Louisa's, Tom's, and Stephen Blackpool's. Although the constant attempts on the part of Bounderby and Gradgrind to brainwash Louisa fail, she falls into a fatalistic malaise of the spirit, eventually allowing her father to bully her into a marriage of convenience with the much older Bounderby. She stays in the marriage at the insistence of her brother, who wants to use her to help him manipulate Bounderby. She comes to know two of the "hands," Stephen and his friend Rachel, and sympathizes with their plight. She also becomes friends with her husband's protégé, the young Harthouse, who falls in love with her. When he tries to seduce her, she returns to her father's house, where she is welcomed with open arms.

Tom, her brother, begins to work for Bounderby about the same time his sister is married to the older man. He becomes thoroughly dissipated, not caring whom he hurts with his reckless gambling. He feels no guilt about draining his sister of her funds to pay his considerable debts and has no compunction about framing Stephen to take the fall for stealing funds that Tom himself has taken. As it becomes obvious, finally, that Tom and not Stephen is the culprit, he is directed by Sissy to hide in the circus, where his father finds him and, with the help of the circus owner, gets him on a ship leaving the country.

Bounderby spends his life lying about his past to build himself up as a self-made man, forcing marriage on the young Louisa, but surrounding himself with fawning scoundrels: Tom, Harthouse, and Mrs. Sparsit. Finally, he is exposed as a fraud by the mother that he had abandoned. He dismisses Mrs. Sparsit, his longtime housekeeper and hostess (who has despised him all along), and dies prematurely and friendless.

Gradgrind, the father of Tom and Louisa, admires the false, blustering Bounderby over all other people. He perpetrates his own set of myths about the supremacy of facts and materialism, and he abets Bounderby in his loveless marriage to Louisa. But Gradgrind has a traumatic epiphany as he comes to terms with Tom's villainy and secretly gets him on a boat before he can be arrested. After this he greatly modifies his old ideas.

Sissy Jupe and Stephen Blackpool are at the center of the important parallel working-class plots. Sissy is abandoned by her father, who is no longer able to thrive as a circus performer. Although Gradgrind deplores the circus and everything it represents, and is apprehensive about the influence Sissy might have on his children, he takes her in. She becomes the humanizing mainstay of the family, but Gradgrind's hope that she will be transformed goes awry when her performance in the school he sponsors, taught by the M'Choakemchilds, continues to be miserably inadequate and she is forced to withdraw. She does not see her circus friends again until she arranges for them to hide Tom from the authorities.

Stephen Blackpool, one of the factory hands, is living in misery, overworked and underpaid by his boss, Bounderby; chained to a drunken wife who appears in town periodically; and forbidden by his situation from marrying the woman he loves, another factory worker named Rachel. Desperate, he approaches Bounderby for advice in dissolving his marriage, but Bounderby expresses outrage, denies him help, and labels him as a troublemaker. To add to his troubles, Rachel has extracted a promise from him to keep removed from any labor disputes, so when one arises and he refuses to become involved, he is outcast by his "brothers." Having heard this rumor, Bounderby sends for him, expecting him to inform on the workers involved in the protest. When Stephen refuses and, moreover, expresses his sympathy for the workers, Bounderby fires him. Louisa, who is present during the conversation, calls on Stephen (with her brother, Tom) that evening to give him money. Tom draws him aside to instruct him to go outside the bank for several evenings to await the promise of a job, thus setting Stephen up as a thief for the robbery that Tom intends to commit. When it becomes apparent that no work is forthcoming, Stephen leaves town. He becomes the main suspect and is asked to return, if he is innocent, to clear up matters, but the community, hearing no word from him, assumes his guilt. On an evening walk, Rachel and Sissy find that Stephen is entrapped in an abandoned shaft called "the Old Hell Shaft," into which he fell on the way back to Coketown. He lives just long enough to say that Tom knows what really happened and to ask the elder Gradgrind to clear his (Stephen's) name.

THE CONTEXT

The setting of *Hard Times* in mid-nineteenth century is a time when the Industrial Revolution had transformed the English landscape, many villages and small subsistent farms having been abandoned as the displaced poor crowded into industrial areas. Dickens had heretofore depicted the urban poor in London, a city not dominated by factories, in works like *Oliver Twist,* about a little boy barely getting enough to eat in an orphanage where children died of disease and starvation and later being enslaved by criminals to work as a petty thief in the streets of London. There is also Bob Cratchit in "A Christmas Carol," overworked and barely keeping his family alive on the wages he is given.

In *Hard Times* Dickens turned his attention to a factory town, that sordid consequence of the Industrial Revolution. Here efficiency, technology, productivity, and profits rose, bringing new status to the factory-owning middle class, while those who actually ran the machinery suffered in every possible way. The wages they had sought by moving to factory towns were too low to subsist on. Figures from the 1860s and 1870s show the average income per week for an entire working-class family to be 31 shillings (roughly $3.72). The average for adult male workers was 19 shillings a week (or a little over two dollars). Because they now lived in towns, separated from nature, the meager diets they could afford could not be augmented by hunting, fishing, or growing some of their food, and artificially inflated prices of wheat (the Corn Laws) contributed to poverty throughout England.

Workers were packed into huge, unsanitary buildings where large families often lived in a single room. Inadequate wages forced all members of the family, some as young as five and six, to work in mills and mines.

The long hours of work required of laborers left them exhausted and in ill health. The new machines not only produced goods at a rapid pace, they also took lives and limbs at a startling rate, a subject that Dickens addressed in some of his newspaper articles. With the combination of over-work, pollution, and danger from machinery, life expectancy was low.

Despite ill health and injuries on the job, the owners paid for no medical care, no job security, no workers' compensation for injuries on the job, and provided no retirement for the elderly or other community services. Any schooling, like the one run by the aptly named Mr. and Mrs. M'Choakumchild, was virtually nonexistent.

Reforms to give workers some modicum of protection were paltry and slow in being introduced. The Reform Act of 1832 extended the suffrage only to 20 percent of the male adult population, including factory owners, not factory workers. In 1833, the year after, Parliament passed the Factory Act, outlawing the employment of children less than nine years of age in silk mills and limiting the working hours of children. The reality was, however, that children under nine were still working in other textile mills and in the mines. Not until 1843 did the government legislate protective laws for children working in the mines. In 1834, Parliament enacted "the new Poor Laws," which proved from the first to be a burden rather than a help for the working poor, in that the government eliminated direct assistance to the poor and, instead, established notoriously squalid institutions to which the poor were consigned. In 1846, two pieces of legislation were passed to alleviate widespread hunger among the working classes and improve working conditions: The Corn Laws, which had artificially inflated the price of grain, were modified, and the workday was limited to ten hours.

It was reformers and working people themselves who were largely responsible for forcing the small improvements in the lives of factory workers, often in the face of violent government reaction. Industrialism was concentrated in the north of England, where in 1819, one of the first major working class rebellions occurred. To pay for the king's Napoleonic Wars, the government had drastically cut services to the workers and the poor. In what was called the Peterloo Massacre, when 60,000 workers demonstrated, they were attacked by police. Eleven workers were killed. Instead of addressing their demands, the government passed six Acts to limit the rights of workers, including their right to assemble.

The 1830s saw the rise of an effective trade union called the Chartists who worked for universal male suffrage at a time when only 20 percent of the adult male population could vote. In the Chartists' protest of 1839, scores were killed and hundreds were injured and arrested. The hordes of union men throughout the country who launched a national wide strike in 1842 were defeated. Fifteen hundred of them were arrested, and 79 were deported to the penal colony, Australia. They again attempted reform in 1848 with little success. As living and working conditions showed little improvement, other local unions were formed: the Amalgamated Association of Cotton Spinners, the Weavers' Union, and the Amalgamated Ironworkers' Association, to name a few. The publications of individuals and smaller groups attempted to call public attention to the problems of the working class. In 1844, a group of English tailors published a report on the contamination of clothing made in city slums, and the next year, Benjamin Disraeli's novel, *Sybil, or the Two Nations,* showed an England sharply divided between the very rich and the very poor. In 1848, Karl Marx and Friedrich Engels published *The Communist Manifesto,* calling for "workers of all countries" to unite: "You have nothing to lose but your chains." In the same year, one of the first novels graphically detailing living and working conditions of workers appeared—Elizabeth Gaskell's *Mary Barton.* And in 1850, Charles Kingsley published two works designed to call attention to the heartbreak and dangers of poverty: a pamphlet titled "Cheap Clothes and Nasty," and a novel, *Alton Locke,* depicting the unsanitary hovels in which sweatshop workers were forced to live.

The immediate event that motivated the writing of *Hard Times* was the 1853 strike and lockout at Preston, a textile-manufacturing town in the north of England. The disruption began when weavers refused as inadequate the owners' offer of a 10 percent raise. When the owners refused to raise wages any higher, many Preston workers in the mills went on strike. In October, the owners declared a lockout, closing all the Preston mills, thereby cutting off all income for all Preston workers, both strikers and nonstrikers. During the eight-month struggle, led by two organizers, the Preston laborers were sustained materially by contributions of money and food from workers in other areas, and spiritually by constant demonstrations, meetings, and encouraging speeches. But in April of 1854, the strike collapsed without the workers having made any gains. And by the beginning of May, 7,700 strikers had returned to their jobs. Their leaders were arrested for conspiracy and later released.

Dickens made a two-day trip to Preston at the height of the strike, in January of 1854, to observe the situation for himself, before writing an article on it, titled "On Strike" for the February 1854 edition of *Household Words*. *Hard Times*, set in a factory town like Preston, appeared in the same year.

The following excerpt from "On Strike" reveals Dickens's impressions of what he saw. The conclusion is somewhat mixed. Although he acknowledges the misery of the working man, he is critical of the labor leaders and deplores the workers' strike as well as the owners' shutout. The first is a speech made by one of the organizers. Dickens includes it in "On Strike," strangely declaring it to be "the worst" of the speeches he heard, containing, he says, some passion certainly, but not much logic or reason:

Friends and Fellow Operatives,

...Your kindness and generosity, your patience and long-continued support deserve every praise, and are only equaled by the heroic and determined perseverance of the outraged and insulted factory workers of Preston, who have been struggling for some months, and are, at this inclement season of the year, bravely battling for the rights of themselves and the whole community.

. . .

This system of giving everything to the few, and nothing to the many, has lasted long enough, and we call upon the working people of this country to be determined to establish a new and improved system—a system that shall give to all who labour, a fair share of those blessings and comforts which their toil produce; in short, we wish to see that divine precept enforced, which says, "Those who will not work, shall not eat."

The task is before you, working men; if you think the good which would result from its accomplishment, is worth struggling for, set to work and cease not, until you have obtained the *good time coming*, not only for the Preston Operatives, but for yourselves as well. [emphasis in original]

By Order of the Committee.
Murphy's Temperance Hotel, Chapel Walks,
Preston, January 24th, 1854

Despite Dickens's disapproval of its revolutionary sentiments, the speech accurately reflects the attitudes of the great mass of workers in England's industrial cities in the north.

THE FACTORY TOWN'S ENVIRONMENT

Dickens develops the characteristics of Coketown largely through the use of metaphor. Its stark, red brick buildings, covered by layers of soot, are like the painted faces of savages. The black smoke that continually boils out of the chimneys is an endless serpent. The deafening machines that work up and down, rattling windows, are like the heads of mad elephants. The factories themselves are citadels, where gases and killing pollutants are bricked in. One brief glimpse inside the factory reveals its unbearable heat and the crashing noise of machines. The two bodies of water in town—a canal and a river—are both thick, black, and purple with foul-smelling dyes. Bounderby says it looks and smells like money.

The factories dictate the atmosphere of the town's living quarters and streets, thrown together hastily and shabbily, without thought to either beauty or comfort. The town streets are unplanned, narrow, dark, dead-end alleys going in all directions. They and the tiny, dark living quarters oppress the workers who have no choice except to live in them.

THE UNION STRUGGLE

Bounderby is not reluctant to express his view of the workers' attempts to better their lives by forming unions or combinations. He is fond of repeating, as he does to Stephen on his first visit, that unhappy workers want "to be set up in a coach and six, and to be fed on turtle soup and venison, with a gold spoon" (57). He later tells Harthouse that this is the single aim of every hand, man, woman, and child. Furthermore, he is convinced that the best way to deal with troublemakers (read union members), is to send them off to a penal colony. The attitude of most mill owners is that if the workers were worth their salt they would go out and inherit a fortune.

At the same time, mill owners like Bounderby claim that they will be ruined when any improvements are suggested, like sending factory children to school, submitting to inspections, preventing accidents, or cutting down on pollution. Faced with any government regulation, they would simply threaten to close their factories, and the terrified "Home Secretary" would tell him to forget any improvements on the laborers' behalf.

Despite the misery that Dickens alludes to and his own firsthand visit to the Preston strike, where he found the strikers and their leaders to be open and reasonable, in *Hard Times* he portrays the union members and, especially their leader Slackbridge, as misguided, hurtful, hotheaded, and full of hot air. Stephen does come to the defense of his miserable fellow workers, calling them decent folk, and he forcefully, though in generalities, speaks of their poverty in a town so rich. He also says it is a painful burden for the workers to have to live with the owners' disparagement and humiliation. It should be up to the owners, he says, but, he informs Bounderby, "the strong hand" (116) would not help the situation, nor will leaving it alone the way it is. Nor will regarding workers as machines and regulating them according to the figures of production. The solution that Dickens puts into Old Stephen's mouth is as naïve as his own espoused solution to the Preston strike and lockout, in "On Strike": The owners, Stephen says, must draw close to the workers, treating them with "kindness and patience and cheery ways" (116). Workers should not take it on themselves to correct the situation by organizing; owners are the ones to remedy it.

Bounderby's reaction to Stephen's candor brings up another labor problem. He and other owners deal with workers they brand as malcontents by firing them and blacklisting them. Although Stephen is by no means a troublemaker, when he refuses to inform on members of the union, Bounderby tells him he is fired. Stephen protests to Bounderby that now he will be blacklisted, and Bounderby, with no regrets whatsoever, hardheartedly agrees. In order to get work after he leaves town, Stephen must assume a different name.

One reference is made to the danger to which workers are subjected in *Hard Times*. Stephen falls into a treacherous chasm called Old Hell Shaft, one of numerous abandoned mines left as dangerous traps after the mines were closed, posing a menace to anyone who strolled in the general area. Stephen eventually dies from his plunge into the shaft. As he himself is dying, he makes reference to the thousands of men and boys who died working in the mines, hoping each day that the government was "not to let their work be murder to 'em," (203) and to those, like himself, whom the mine kills even after it is no longer in use.

Inequality under the law is a constant source of misery for the workers who see that the law is different for those with the money to manipulate it. Stephen, saddled with an alcoholic wife, is tortured with having to sleep in the same one-room flat with her when she returns to him periodically. Bounderby, who castigates Stephen for his desire to get a divorce, tells him that he might be able to get around the law if he could come up with £1,500 or more.

An equally cruel inequality affects rich and poor criminals. Stephen, if he were tried and convicted of thievery, would be hung. But Gradgrind has the money to buy his son, Tom, a trip out of the country where he will escape prosecution.

LAISSEZ-FAIRE ECONOMICS, MECHANIZATION, AND UTILITARIANISM

Many critics have labeled *Hard Times* a disappointment because Dickens not only generalizes the plight of factory workers, without providing graphic details of their living situations or conditions within the factory, but he also fails to understand the necessity for union activity and strong union leaders to improve their lives. Critics have argued that he may not have had a full grasp of situations in northern factory towns, and, it has been observed, his famous visit to the Preston strike area was only for 48 hours, during which time he entered neither a factory nor the living quarters of any worker.

But Dickens was operating on a more philosophical plane in concentrating on ideas that the Industrial Revolution had proliferated—ideas that had had a detrimental effect on all segments of the population, workers included. In Book One he develops the aspects of laissez-faire, mechanization, utilitarianism, and materialism that are "sown" in society—ideas from which disaster will be "reaped" in Book Two.

Especially detrimental to workers is laissez-faire, or "leave alone," economics that operated on the assumption that the best economic policy for the entire country was to allow industrialists and other businesspersons to conduct their affairs without interference from the government or other agencies, without restrictions, for example, on their pollution of the air and water, and without regulation of workers' hours or salaries, child labor, or safety.

Other overlapping philosophical schools that had sprung up in the wake of the Industrial Revolution were Utilitarianism, materialism, and mechanization. Utilitarianism valued only what was of practical use, devaluing poetry and art. Materialism was elevated to the exclusion of heart, emotions, spirit, and soul. Mechanization defined all things in relation to the machine, until humans themselves were not only dominated by machines but became machines themselves. Dickens singled out for parody particular aspects of these schools of thought, which were the seeds of disaster in the novel.

The novel opens in the school, sponsored by Gradgrind, where the ideas of the Industrial Revolution are disseminated. Here even his own children are taught the supremacy of scientific and mathematical, measurable facts to the absolute exclusion of all else: fancy, emotion, imagination, art, entertainments. This denies individuals their full humanity by suppressing a large part of what it means to be human. "In this life," he tells the students, "we want nothing but facts" (5). Gradgrind, "a man of realities" (6), wants to blow the students "clean out of the regions of childhood" and to provide them with a "grim mechanical substitute for the tender young imaginations" (6). "No little Gradgrind had ever seen a face in the moon" (11). In the classroom, the students learn, for example, that the "truth" of a horse or the true definition of a horse is its cold scientific category: "Quadruped, Graminivorous," not a living fellow creature with whom one interacts.

Even love is beside the point, as Louisa learns in her conversation with her father when he pushes her into marriage with a repulsive man more than twice her age.

Anything not of practical use is forbidden—not poetry, not fairy tales, not "silly" songs like "Twinkle, Twinkle, Little Star," not the representation of nature on such things as wallpaper, not any leisure time entertainments like the circus. The aptly named schoolmaster, M'Choakumchild, has as his aim to "kill outright the robber Fancy" (10).

Sissy Jupe, the young girl reared in the circus, where she was encouraged to enjoy childhood and to read myths and fairy tales, is the antithesis of the values of the Industrial Revolution. She is the heart that holds the Gradgrind family together, but she is incapable of thinking the way M'Choakumchild and Gradgrind insist she must. So, she remains human and in adulthood tries hard to "know her humbler fellow creatures, and to beautify their lives of machinery and reality with those imaginative graces and delights" (222).

Dickens seems to have gotten Gradgrind's view of education from several reliable sources, including a popular textbook titled *A Series of Lessons in Prose and Verse*, published in 1831 by J.M. M'Culloch. The following Gradgrind-like concepts are from the preface to his book:

[A] better order of times has now dawned; and the increased demand which has arisen, within the last few years, for Classbooks compiled on more simple and natural principle, seems to justify the hope,—that the artificial system is on the wane,—that the success of the experiments recently made … is beginning to be admitted,—and that the time is nearly gone by, when children of seven and eight years of age are to be compelled to waste their time and their faculties on such preposterous and unsuitable exercises as enacting dramatic scenes, reciting parliamentary speeches, and reading the latest sentimental poetry. . . .

The following little Work ... has been compiled on the principle
of admitting only such lessons as appeared well adapted to stimulate
juvenile curiosity, and store the mind with useful knowledge. Simple
extracts, relating to Natural History, Elementary Science, Religion,
etc., have taken the place of Dramatic Scenes, Sentimental Poetry,
and parliamentary Orations.(2)

The effect of this kind of education, according to Dickens, is to forbid
children their full humanity, to stunt or suppress compassion and understanding, important parts of their natural humanity, and turn them into
money-making machines like the school's one truly successful student,
Bitzer, who becomes an amoral monster of self-interest. When he comes
to take Tom to be arrested, Gradgrind asks him if he has no heart, to
which Bitzer replies, "The circulation, sir, ... couldn't be carried on
without one" (212). He is acting according to the training he got in
Gradgrind's school, which taught that:

[E]verything was to be paid for. Nobody was ever on any account to
give anybody anything, or render anybody help without purchase.
Gratitude was to be abolished, and the virtues springing from it
were not to be. Every inch of the existence of mankind, from birth
to death, was to be a bargain across a counter. And if we didn't get
to Heaven that way, it was not a politico-economical place, and we
had no business there. (215)

Gradgrind's philosophy also creates Tom, the self-interested reprobate,
who pushes his sister into a loveless marriage, drains her of her money,
and then frames a helpless worker for his own crime.

The immediate effect of these schools of philosophy and this education
on the workers is that it trains members of the ruling class who have and
will have complete control over the factories, the factory towns, and the
workers' lives. The owners are trained to make decisions without moral
considerations. Their sole interest will be accumulating capital by pro-
moting what is useful, efficient, and profitable.

To the owners, the workers are not fully human; they are hands. They
are measured in terms of what they can produce. Each is a unit of so much
horsepower. For this reason, society denies them everything but work.
Their work lives are unrelieved by leisure or beauty or sentiment. They

emerge from the factory and go to their grim quarters, where they collapse from weariness. The author warns the community:

> Cultivate in them, while there is yet time, the utmost graces of the fancies and affections, to adorn their lives so much in need of ornament; or, in the day of your triumph, when romance is utterly driven out of their souls, and they and a bare existence stand face to face, Reality will take a wolfish turn, and make an end of you! (125)

But although fancy, beauty, art, and cheerfulness might be essential to fulfilling a worker's life, the ability of these attributes to solve the problems of hunger and overwork created by the Industrial Revolution are highly questionable.

Eventually, Gradgrind, at least, comes to a partial realization that his theories and view of education were not to be taken without a grain of salt. "Faith, Hope, and Charity" (221) lead him to bend his facts and figures, and he atones somewhat for his past by distributing broadsides that exonerate the wronged factory worker, Stephen Blackpool, and place the guilt on his privileged son, Tom.

HARD TIMES ISSUES IN THE TWENTY-FIRST CENTURY

Working-class issues raised in *Hard Times* resonate in the twentieth and twenty-first century United States. Facets of laissez-faire economics surface persistently, arguing that industry and business must be free to operate without constraints and that what is good for business is good for everyone. In the resulting unrestricted pursuit of capital, the worker is without protections. In the Eisenhower administration, the mantra of Charles Wilson, former head of General Motors, was "What's good for General Motors is good for the country." In the Reagan administration, the label was "trickle-down economics." And in the George W. Bush administration, it manifested itself in massive tax breaks for the wealthy, forcing cuts in workers' social services and education.

The issue of safety in the workplace, despite massive, federally decreed regulations, still plagues workers in the twenty-first century. For example, newspapers reported that a highly respected company with factories throughout the country had neglected safety regulations, leading to the death and maiming of its employees. In another instance, in a chicken processing factory in North Carolina, workers died in a fire because the exits were locked. And the refusal of agribusinesses to allow farm workers to seek shelter during the hottest hours of the day leads to the persistence of heatstroke and skin cancer.

Union membership and retaliation against workers remain as issues, even in the twenty-first century. Even though the right to join a union is technically a part of U.S. law, retaliation against union members and whistle-blowers continues. University issued studies in 2003 indicated the frequency with which employers fire workers who participate in union organizing. As a common practice, companies keep consultants on their staff to develop strategies to fight unionization.

Another workplace issue raised by *Hard Times* is contemporary to the twenty-first century: this is factory pollution, which not only impinges on the global environment, but especially effects workers inside the plants and their families who live in close proximity to the workplace. In 1999 the government passed what was called the "New Source Review" requiring factory owners to put in place equipment to control pollution whenever they did factory upgrades. But in 2002, this new rule was gutted, as loopholes were introduced to allow upgrades without requiring new pollution controls.

Although Dickens's proposed solution to the problems of the working class might have been less than effective, the issues he raised in *Hard Times* have never been dated and are as relevant in the twenty-first century as they were in 1854.

QUESTIONS AND PROJECTS

1. Have a debate on the question of Dickens's attitude toward unions and worker resistance. Do you agree with his implied position on unions and strikes?
2. Write a characterization of James Harthouse. In the end, is he an honorable or a dishonorable character? Be sure to consider his name. How, from your reading, does Dickens judge him?
3. Write an essay on Dickens's presentation of social problems created by the factory system.
4. Do you find Gradgrind's conversion to be believable? Have a discussion on the question.
5. Write an essay on Dickens's choice of names in *Hard Times* and what they imply.

6. Write and stage a one-act play showing an hour in M'Choakumchild's school. Choose the characters, even creating some, if you wish, and writing lines that deal with the "fact versus fancy" philosophy.
7. Analyze Sissy Jupe's answers to the schoolmaster's questions. Write a paper on it, which includes the truth we see in how she responds and her position in opposition to the Gradgrind theory.
8. Have a discussion on the effect of Dickens's inclusion of Gradgrind's successful attempt to get his son out of the country.
9. Conduct research and make a report on the thought of Adam Smith or Jeremy Bentham.
10. Interview an educator who holds a master's degree in education. Ask your subject questions about philosophies of education, how educational philosophy has changed over the years, and what he or she regards as the strong and weak points of each.

FURTHER READING

Barnard, Robert. *Imagery and Theme in the Novels of Dickens.* Universitesforlaget: Norwegian University Press, 1974.

Beauchamp, Gorman. "Mechanomorphism in *Hard Times*," *Studies in the Literary Imagination* 22:1 (Spring 1989): 61–77.

Butterworth, R.D. "Dickens the Novelist: The Preston Strike and *Hard Times*," *Dickensian* 88:2 (Summer 1992): 91–102.

Dickens, Charles. *Hard Times.* New York: W.W. Norton and Company, 2001.

Glancy, Ruth. A *Student Companion to Charles Dickens.* Westport, CT: Greenwood Publishing, 1999.

Hollington, Michael, ed. *Charles Dickens.* Sussex: Helm Information, 1995.

Johnson, Patricia E. "*Hard Times* and the Structure of Industrialism: The Novel as Factory," *Studies in the Novel* 21:2 (1989): 128–37.

Jordan, John O., ed. *The Cambridge Companion to Charles Dickens.* Cambridge: Cambridge University Press, 2001.

Kelly, John. *Charles Dickens in the Literary Criticism of F.R. Leavis.* Roma: Marra Editions, 1989.

Newsom, Robert. *Charles Dickens Revisited.* New York: Twayne Publishers, 2000.

Page, Norman, ed. *Dickens' Hard Times, Great Expectations, and* Our Mutual Friend: *A Casebook*. London: Macmillan, 1979.

Pykett, Lyn. *Charles Dickens*. New York: Palgrave, 2002.

Rooke, Patrick. *The Age of Dickens*. London: Wayland, 1970.

Saunders, Andrew. *Charles Dickens*. New York: Oxford University Press, 2003.

3

Herman Melville's "The Paradise of Bachelors and the Tartarus of Maids"

One year before Dickens published *Hard Times*, his condemnation of the fruits of the Industrial Revolution, Herman Melville wrote a single short fiction consisting of two contrasting sketches, "The Paradise of Bachelors and the Tartarus of Maids." Whereas Dickens's *Hard Times* concentrates on life outside the workplace and speaks of the inside of the factory in generalities, Melville provides the reader with one of the most graphic, meticulously detailed fictional pictures of the inside of a nineteenth-century American factory. The sketch, first published in *Harper's* in 1855, has been read from a variety of perspectives by its critics: as Melville's autobiography, as primarily a sexual commentary, as a comment on the human condition, and as a condemnation of the work conditions perpetuated by the Industrial Revolution, which only reached the United States in the nineteenth century. In keeping with the character of this volume, the essay at hand will take the last approach. As Marvin Fisher writes in *Going Under*:

> Only Melville, ... among his nineteenth-century contemporaries, responded so dramatically, casting the system of the machine in opposition to warmth, comfort, to health and beauty, to love and sympathy, to individualism and pride in craftsmanship, to free will, or to any sense of harmony with nature. It threatened every physical, psychological, organic, and spiritual attribute of humanity. (Fisher 93)

The workplace issues in the sketch are fundamental and numerous: the physical danger of the workplace, the dehumanization of women workers by the machine, the physical and spiritual poverty of the workers who seem little more than slaves, the demeaning and denaturing of the workers by the factory system, and the contrast between the lives of working women and men.

The first half of the sketch, "The Paradise of Bachelors," inspired by Melville's four-day visit to the Inns of Court in December 1849, takes place in ancient sequestered buildings in London called the Temple, which serve primarily as law offices but also contain some apartments for unmarried lawyers. The second half, titled "The Tartarus of Maids," is based on Melville's visit to Carson's Old Red Paper Mill in Dalton, Massachusetts in January of 1851. The focal point of the fiction, viewed as social commentary, is "The Tartarus of Maids," with "The Paradise of Bachelors" serving as an instructive contrast to the misery of the New England workers. Although one must keep in mind that the two sketches are inextricably linked and that aspects of the London lawyers' workplace and quarters are presented in contrast to that of the maids, for clarity's sake, the plot and context of each sketch is treated separately in the following discussion.

THE NARRATIVE: "THE PARADISE OF BACHELORS"

"The Paradise of Bachelors" does not have the traditional rising action of a conventional plot. Rather, it is a portrait of a small society of privileged individuals and their surroundings, culminating in the consuming of a sumptuous dinner to which the American narrator has been invited. The sketch opens as the narrator, having left his hotel in Trafalgar Square, strolls down London's busy streets and turns into an enclosed, peaceful garden. As he walks through the grounds toward his lawyer host's apartment, he compares and contrasts the present residents of the "Temple" with the medieval monastic knights who once occupied it. After arriving at his host's apartment, he describes in detail the various courses served at dinner and the demeanor and conversation of the nine bachelors present. The sketch ends as the guests depart, arm in arm.

The portrait of the bachelors and their paradise is painted with the heavy use of imagery and allusion, beginning with the title itself, which declares the bachelors' secluded workplace to be a paradise. The surroundings of their workplace are designed to cultivate the intellect and to invite the soul: landscaped parks, terraces, gardens, and flower beds; riverside benches; a church and cloisters; fine libraries—all in stark contrast to the dark, ugly haphazard streets and hovels of Dickens's London and his fictional Coketown, as well as the stark icy environment the narrator describes in "The Tartarus of Maids."

Unlike the workers in *Hard Times* and "The Tartarus of Maids," those who are members of the Temple live chiefly to consume, not to produce. They are famous, not so much for the cases they present at the bar, as for the dinner parties they host and enjoy in their apartments.

The stories told around the table confirm the privileged status of the bachelors. Unlike members of the working class, they have been afforded the finest of educations. Whereas poverty has left members of the working class with insufficient food, the lawyers enjoy lavish feasts. And whereas long hours of killing work have left workers without leisure, these men in the Temple spend their time amusing themselves. The men around the opulent dinner table speak of their Oxford educations, their frequent European travel, and the time spent in study in the British Museum.

THE CONTEXT

The Inns of Court, located in London and adjoining Westminster, control legal matters in Britain, including legal education and admission to the bar. Barristers (those of the highest degree in Britain's legal system) have offices here, assisted by an army of solicitors and clerks. At the time of Melville's sketch, many barristers also lived within the walls of one of the Inns of Court. There are four distinct Inns of Court. The first two, Inner Temple and Middle Temple, are in a common area known as the Temple, located in an area near Fleet Street, on the border between London and Westminster. (This is the setting of "The Paradise of Bachelors.") The other two Inns of Court—Lincoln's Inn and Gray's Inn—are in Westminster. The Inner and Middle Temples have an ancient, distinguished history. As late in the nineteenth century as the setting of Melville's "The Paradise of Bachelors," only male members of a small favored class in England were admitted to the bar as barristers. These men were usually from wealthy, titled families and did not need to work to support themselves. Although only members of the bar had offices in the Inns of Court, the segment of the population there did little legal work.

An examination of the larger picture of life in England in the 1830s, 1840s, and early 1850s reveals just how far removed from the world life at the Inns of Court was. At the time of Melville's visit there, poverty was widespread in England as more and more people were displaced from the land and unable to farm, and the jobs that were available paid only starvation wages. In 1850, for example, the year before Melville visited the Inns of Court, the average weekly salary in an English textile mill was slightly over nine shillings a week (roughly equivalent to one U.S. dollar a week). In 1845, the number of paupers in England was more than a million and a half people. The attitude toward the masses of poor is illustrated by the Poor Laws, passed by Parliament in 1834 to tighten up relief for the poor. These laws, which emphasized the place of workhouses in the solution, were regarded as attacks on the poor. The express purpose was to give no relief except to inmates of the workhouses and to make life in the workhouses more unpleasant than any situation to be met with outside the workhouse. Living conditions and work in the workhouses were more onerous, and families were segregated there, to prevent the conception of children.

At midcentury, the average annual income for the comparable few members of the upper class was more than £5,000, leaving them money to invest capital in new industries and eventually make more money. At the same time, women who were fortunate enough to find work in mills were making on average of seven shillings, or about 84 cents a week or $300 a year.

Melville was in part presenting the difference between the poverty-stricken masses and the privileged few (like the residents of the Inns of Court) in terms of food consumption. The focus of "The Paradise of Bachelors" is a nine-course feast. At the same time, the masses in England were slowly emerging from what has been called "the Hungry Forties," so named because of the intense poverty and starvation among the working classes, caused chiefly by the British Corn Laws. As far back as the fifteenth century, Corn Laws had been passed solely to keep the price of all grains high enough for the British gentry, who grew them, to make a fat profit. Theses laws specifically forbid the import of foreign grains at competitive prices. The poor, who needed to buy grain to make their bread, could scarcely afford it. The result was an intensification of the already sharp division between rich and poor. Not until 1846, near the end of the brutal Hungry Forties, were the Corn Laws repealed, probably after tales of wrenching hunger reached the halls of Parliament. For example, Parliament heard the case of paupers in Andover, England, who were hired to crush bones and were so hungry that they fought one another for the rotting gristle remaining on the horses' bones. This was in 1847, just four years before Melville's feast in the Temple. Workers fared little better than paupers. In a court case in the mid-1840s, a witness noted that women and men doing long hours of backbreaking work in the mills lived on only one meager meal a day. To deepen the context of class difference in terms of feasts and starvation, it is instructive to turn to Melville's "Poor Man's Pudding and Rich Man's Crumbs," which is based on his own experience in London in 1849. He travels through "squalid lanes" to a "dirty blind alley," where the leftover food from a banquet had been dumped for the poor to consume. Foreign ministers and members of the nobility had been present at the banquet. Now the poor fight over the remains of the half-eaten feast.

THE MEANING OF PARADISE

But the bachelors are far removed from the misery and starvation on the "squalid lanes" of London that Melville had described in his 1849 journal as being like the Pit of Hell. Instead, the bachelors live in Paradise. The first definition of *Paradise*, given in the definitive *Oxford English Dictionary*, equates it with the biblical Garden of Eden. What are its characteristics? And what is its relevance to Melville's sketch? The real world, which Adam and Eve enter after they are banished from Paradise, serves as a negative definition of Paradise by indicating what it is *not*. The fundamental contrast between Paradise and the outside world is the different element of time. In Paradise, time stands still. Things always remain the same. People do not change, grow up, and grow old. Their surroundings remain familiar, eternally, comfortably the same.

It is only with the fall that full adulthood, sex, childbirth, children, and family become part of Adam and Eve's lives. After the fall, these things come to define what it means to be fully human.

Among the chief curses of the fallen world are work and responsibility. In Paradise, Adam and Eve played among nature and had no idea of arduous work. But after being thrown out of the Garden of Eden's protective walls, they are cursed with hard physical labor to provide themselves with shelter, food, clothing, and protection from the now-hostile animals and human enemies.

The Temple pretends to be a Paradise before the fall. Time seems to have stood still in their opulent gardens, which have changed little since the days of the medieval knights who once lived there. The beautiful grounds are protectively surrounded by walls that shut out the world of hard work created by the Industrial Revolution (unlike the lawyer's

American workplace in Melville's "Bartleby the Scrivener"). Here, where time has stood still, in a setting that seems hardly a workplace at all, the inhabitants are exempt from having to work with their hands, secluded from the world of the machine and the Industrial Revolution that brings misery to the New England factory worker.

The Temple was once the monastery of the Knights Templar, an order of religious militants who fought in the Crusades but ended in moral decay. By contrast, the lawyers who live and work here in the nineteenth century are sedentary, inactive men who seem to cause more obstruction than production in their work of providing legal advice and preparing cases to argue at court: Their "particular charge" is to "check, to clog, to hinder and embarrass all the courts and avenues of Law" (263), and who are more eagerly occupied with lavish wining, dining, and socializing.

The passage of time has not brought the bachelors into full adulthood. Here they are free of domestic responsibility. Their lives are in contrast to the American Benedicks (usually meaning newly married tradesmen) who must worry about "the rise of bread and the fall of babies":

> It was the very perfection of quiet absorption of good living, good drinking, good feeling, and good talk. We were a band of brothers. Comfort—fraternal, household comfort, was the grand trait of the affair. Also, you could plainly see that these easy-hearted men had no wives or children to give an anxious thought. Almost all of them were travelers, too; for bachelors alone can travel freely, and without any twinges of their consciences touching desertion of the fireside. (269)

THE IRONY OF PARADISE

But Melville is ironic in his comparison of the bachelor's quarters to Paradise, for, since the fall, true Paradise does not really exist; there can be only a pretense of Eden. In the first place, there is the pretense that Eden is characterized by all that is natural, whereas, after the fall, nature and natural truth live only in the fallen world to which mankind has been consigned. The implication from this is that the bachelors, free of heterosexuality, love, or domesticity, are living unnatural lives.

Paradise is a self-gratifying deception, an egocentric delusion of purity and universal happiness. Those who pretend, in this fallen world, to live in Eden suppress their own full humanity. In the nineteenth-century tales and novels of Melville's close friend, Nathaniel Hawthorne, such people who live lies bring destruction on themselves and others. The deluded villains in Hawthorne's stories are often single men who have resisted commitment to women and escaped the responsibility of families—characters like Dimmesdale in *The Scarlet Letter*, Coverdale in *The Blithedale Romance*, and the Reverend Hooper in "The Minister's Black Veil." Melville portrays the bachelors of the Temple in the same vein. They are more like little well-behaved boys, wrapped up in the good life of self-gratification.

Here are a group of privileged and inattentive men who carry out their lives of self-indulgence while blind to, even staunchly denying, the reality that the vast majority of people in the world live in pain and suffering:

> The thing called pain, the bugbear styled trouble—those two legends seemed preposterous to their bachelor imaginations. How could men of liberal sense, ripe scholarship in the world, and capacious philosophical and convivial understandings—how could they suffer themselves to be imposed upon by such monkish fables? Pain! Trouble! As well talk of Catholic miracles. No such thing.—Pass the sherry, sir.—Pooh, pooh! Can't be!—The port, sire, if you please. Nonsense: don't tell me so.—The decanter stops with you, sir, I believe. (269)

They are incapable of acknowledging that their comfort is made possible only through the killing labor of others in the real world. A single reference to Southern plantation life hilariously underscores the absurdity and cruelty of the pretense of living in Eden at the expense of their fellow men. As the narrator contemplates the "snug" bachelor apartments, the "dear delightful spot," and the "sweet hours there passed," he is inexplicably reminded "through poetry" of the song, "'Carry me back to Old Virginny!'"—initially inexplicable because the Temple is all genteel English decorum and the song is from an American blackface minstrel show, written in 1847 by the white minstrel man E. P. Christy. (The version more familiar to twentieth-century audiences was published by James A. Bland in 1878, well after Melville wrote his sketch.) The "Virginny" the minstrel sings about and comes to the narrator's mind in London is a plantation society where life, on the surface, is romantic and comfortable and genteel, much in the spirit of the life lived by the London bachelors. But underneath that comfort, supporting it and making it possible, is a vast population of black slaves. The puzzling connection between the bachelor lawyers in London and the Southern population of plantation owners and slaves in a minstrel show song, "Ole Virginny" lends a laughable absurdity to the comparison. But the reader is still obliged to wonder why Melville makes the connection. The answer links the two parts of the sketch, that is, the bachelors' lives of luxury and ease (like those of the plantation owners) to those of the vast population of hard-laboring factory slaves, like the consumptive maids in the New England paper mill.

THE NARRATIVE: "THE TARTARUS OF MAIDS"

The bachelors' Paradise is a rosy, superficial world, beneath which lies, in stark contrast, the grim *Tartarus* (meaning hell) of maids. The Oxford English Dictionary defines *Tartarus* as the depths of the infernal place, usually called hell. (It should be noted here that the nineteenth century was the age of euphemism, when neutral terms were substituted for what were regarded as unpleasant words. The word *hell* was regarded as unfit for polite society, so *Tartarus* was frequently substituted for it.) Dante, whom Melville mentions, contributed details to the Western World tradition of hell. His inferno consisted of descending circles. The damned in the topmost circles suffered the least serious punishment, whereas those in the lowest rings endured the most horrific. As the narrator describes the increasing, unbearable cold as he descends to the factory, one is reminded that the lowest rung of Dante's hell is not flame but solid ice. The plot proceeds as the narrator, like a nineteenth-century Dante, gradually makes his descent into the center of hell—the factory—through which he is given a tour.

The language and imagery he uses to describe his journey underscore his impression that the workplace of the maids in the paper mill is not only in hell, but that it is in the worst, lowest ring of hell. The narrator, a "seedsman" who needs paper envelops to send his wares throughout the country, is a thinly veiled version of Melville, the writer, who needs paper to broadcast his prose and poetry. Although it is January, the narrator declares that he has left "bright farms and sunny meadows" to gradually descend into an excruciating cold so extreme that his cheeks become frostbitten. The language, leaving no doubt that this is hellish territory includes terms like "cloven walls" (like the devil's hoofs), the nearby "Woedolor Mountains," the "violent" Gulf Stream, "Mad Maid's Bellow pipe," a "Dantean" gateway, the "ebon" or black colors, the "Black Notch," the word "Plutonian," an adjective describing the underworld, a hollow called "the Devil's Dungeon," a fallen tree that looks like a giant serpent, and the pass between the mountains that are Alpine "corpses."

The plot takes the narrator from room to room in the paper mill: the folding room; the room where the water wheel turns; the rag room; the pulp room; and, finally, the room where the enormous main machine is housed. The plot's climax occurs as the narrator almost faints at the idea of the machine's mindless supremacy over the girls. In the tale's denouement, the narrator learns further details about the girls and their work and leaves, returning home from hell.

THE CONTEXT

This tale of the women workers in a small paper mill is set near the beginning of the Industrial Revolution in the United States, which brought with it innovative technology, mass production, radical new methods of efficiency, and new kinds and uses of power. The real age of the machine reached the northeast shores of the United States in the first decades of the nineteenth century. Work moved away from home industries and small shops to factory towns. At first there were small factories, like Carson's Red Paper Mill, in small villages. These small operations continued. Then in 1814, Francis Cabot Lowell pirated the power loom technology from England and built the first mill, making use of the new technology in Waltham, Massachusetts. After his death in 1817, his friends and family began the construction of what would be the first genuine mill town in 1824, named Lowell in his honor, on the banks of the Merrimack River, north of Boston. Lowell and its sister town of Lawrence were similar to Dickens's Coketown in general concept, but the differences were substantial, in that the Lowell owners, particularly, attempted to mitigate the hard work with lectures and musical performances and to plan an orderly, attractive town and dormitories. Some of the earlier textile mills (including the one at Waltham) hired entire families, from six-year-olds to adults. Within a few years, however, most workers in the mills were girls and women. Indeed, the new textile mill procedures were specifically designed for women workers. Although textile mills predominated, other industries also used women workers exclusively in the making of pottery, pencils, watches, matches, clocks, and—the subject of Melville's sketch—paper. So throughout the nineteenth century, young women, reared on farms, left to work in mills far from home.

The reasons given for the hiring of women were many—some practical, some actually theological. (They were also the same reasons given for the hiring of children as young as six years.) The United States was still an agrarian society, and most of the male citizens were still farmers.

By hiring women, especially the daughters of farmers, to work in the new factories, the men would still be left free to farm. Moreover, women could be hired to work for much lower salaries, leading to much higher profits for factory owners. In a government-issued report on factories in 1821, the happy conclusion drawn was that a factory could make a surplus profit of $14,000 each year for every 200 women it hired instead of men. The practice of hiring women in factories was a boon to the farmers as well as to the factory owners because it was expected that the women's wages would be used to pay off their fathers' mortgages and put their brothers through college.

The profit motive was, as always, the bottom line, and it was conveniently buttressed by the Calvinistic view of women and of idleness. Idleness was regarded by the New England Puritan as the supreme sin, of the lower classes in particular, for God had called each individual to a particular work that strengthened the whole of a godly community. Combined with that was the prevailing view of women, thought to be weak in every way—morally, intellectually, and psychologically. They were (Melville raises the point in "The Paradise of Maids"), in effect, eternally children, or girls. One of the greatest dangers to society was an idle woman who was, by reason of her idleness, prone to vice and mischief and became a drain on her father or the public coffers.

The historic move from the home farm to the factory was a traumatic one for young women in that they were no longer surrounded by supportive, sympathetic families and communities. And, for the first time, they were obliged to take orders from factory bosses. What they lost in emotional, familial support, they gained in a degree of independence. Some thrived on their new independence and introduction to a world larger than the family farm.

The textile industry was extensive, far exceeding other factory work. And the surviving "Lowell girl" diaries, letters home, and articles in the worker-produced *The Lowell Offering* provide a rich picture of nineteenth-century factory life in general, most of which is germane to paper mills and other factories run with machinery. Other information about life working in factories is provided by government reports, many provoked by mill worker protests. Melville would have known about an 1836 demonstration in Lowell (considered the first major labor protest in the United States), when 1,500 women walked off the job, the formation of the Lowell Female Labor Reform organization in 1844, as well as reports and arguments that led to the passage of the 10-hour work day in 1847 (a law that was essentially ignored until 1874).

The average weekly income for all female factory workers was four or five dollars a week. Out of this they paid $3.50 a week for room and board, if they were not housed in company dormitories.

The living situation of female workers in the "model" community of Lowell was scarcely ideal. Some 600,000 girls between the ages of 10 and 16 years worked in the textile industry in the 1820s and as late as the turn of the century, Lowell hired 1,000 girls under the age of 16 years. The dormitories were usually three stories tall. Eight workers shared one small room, crammed with beds, chairs, trunks, boxes, desks, and clothing. In addition, each bed was shared by two or three women. Problems of compatibility were persistent and bothersome. There was no indoor plumbing and the outdoor privies continually polluted the workers' drinking water. Nor was there any provision for bathing. Maintaining hygiene by hauling in bathwater to a crowded room, shared by seven other workers, was arduous. If this was the highly touted model living situation in Lowell, how much more unpleasant were the dormitories provided for less benevolent owners of places like Carson's Red Paper Mill?

Records from Lowell also indicate something of the working conditions in most mills, where seats were not provided for most workers, who were on their feet the livelong day, except when they sat on the floor of the factory to eat their lunches.

The length of the work day was always a bone of contention in Lowell and other mills. Despite the federal law limiting the work day to 10 hours, factory owners consistently ignored it with impunity. Factory women typically continued to work 14 hours a day, from five in the morning until seven at night. Women in the Fall River, Massachusetts, textile mills reportedly worked 15 hours or more. These were longer days than the "Old Bach" owner of Melville's paper mill admits to requiring, leading the reader to wonder if Melville intended to leave the impression that the proprietor is lying to those outsiders who visit the plant.

Health and safety were issues of utmost importance throughout New England's factory system. In textile mills and in the main machine room of Carson's Red Paper Mill, a high level of humidity was maintained to keep materials in more workable condition. As a consequence, windows were nailed shut. Ventilation was notoriously poor. This high humidity resulted in serious respiratory ailments, including what were then the fatal diseases of consumption, influenza, and typhoid fever. At midcentury it was found that one-half of 1,600 patients, treated annually at the Lowell hospital, had typhoid fever from poor ventilation.

In textile and paper mills, the constant breathing of lint led to consumption. Workers would be covered from head to toe with lint and were said to have continually coughed up lint from their lungs. This accounts for the chalky complexions of the girls in the paper mills. The lint damaged their lungs. The majority of girls who had left home to work in the mills were eventually forced to return for reasons of health, and 70 percent of mill workers in the early decades of the nineteenth century died of respiratory diseases.

Working close to the machinery, with no safety provisions enforced, presented a constant danger to workers. Many women returned home, having lost arms or legs. Some were scalped by the machine. In a horrific 1893 account of industrial accidents, at a time when a number of abuses from the midcentury had been eliminated, Helen Campbell reported on factory work conditions of female workers:

> Some were in ... basements where dampness was added to cold and bad air.... In one case girls were working in "little pens all shelved over.... There are no conveniences for women; and men and women use the same closets, washbasins, and drinking cups, etc." ... In another a water closet in the center of the room filled it with a sickening stench.... Feather-sorters, fur-workers, cotton-sorters, all workers on any material that gives off dust, are subject to lung and bronchial troubles. In soap factories the girls' hands are eaten by the caustic soda, and by the end of the day the fingers are often raw and bleeding. In making buttons, pins, and other manufactures ... there is always liability of getting the fingers jammed or caught. For the first three times the wounds are dressed without charge. After that the person injured must pay expenses....
>
> In match-factories ... necrosis often attacks the worker, and the jaw is eaten away. (Campbell 216–22)

Specific information on conditions in paper mills is scarce, but it is clear that most of the paper mills were in western Massachusetts at that time. The one Melville visits was in Dalton, a few miles from his home in Pittsfield. The most prominent paper mills were located in Holyoke, Massachusetts, not far from South Hadley, the home of Mount Holyoke Seminary, the first institution of higher learning for women and one that encouraged the attendance of mill women. At the turn of the twentieth century, there were 3,000 workers in the 28 mills located in Holyoke. Rag pickers in these mills earned from 80 cents to a dollar a day at mid-nineteenth century. Other paper mill workers at Holyoke earned an average of 75 cents a week plus board.

Paper mill workers suffered from the high humidity. (Cupid, the narrator's young tour guide, suspects that the narrator is suffering from the high heat maintained in the machine room.) They were damaged as well by the lint constantly in the air, in the same way that textile mill workers were. But, in addition, paper mill workers were infected with the contaminated rags that were processed into paper, and they were poisoned by the chemicals used in paper making—both sulfites and bleach.

THE VITAL CONNECTION BETWEEN PARADISE AND TARTARUS

To cement the connection between the Paradise of the London bachelors and the Hell of the maids, in this second section, the narrator makes repeated reference to the first section. Coming from the bustling thoroughfare to the community built around the paper mill, he is reminded of "my first sight of dark and grimy Temple Bar" (275). As his horse dashes through the notch, putting the narrator's life in peril, he is reminded of being on a runaway London bus going under the arches designed by Christopher Wren (275). At his first sight of the factory, he is somehow reminded of the Temple:

> So that, when upon reining up at the protruding rock I at last caught sight of the quaint groupings of the factory-buildings, and with the traveled highway and the Notch behind, found myself all alone, silently and privily stealing through deep-cloven passages into this sequestered spot, and saw the long, high-gabled main factory edifice, with a rude tower—for hoisting heavy boxes—at one end, standing among its crowded outbuilding and boarding-houses, as the Temple Church amidst the surrounding offices and dormitories, and when the marvelous retirement of this mysterious nook fastened its whole spell on me, then, what memory lacked, all tributary imagination furnished, and I said to myself, 'This is the very counterpart of the Paradise of Bachelors, but snowed upon, and frost-painted to a sepulcher.' (275)

Like Temple Bar, the paper mill is sequestered and retiring, but at bottom, it is "an inverted similitude" (276). Everything here is opposite of the bachelor's paradise. In contrast to the "sweet, tranquil Temple

Garden with its green beds," there is a square piled "high with wood, frozen horse post and frost everywhere" (276).

Then he asks, "Where are the gay bachelors?" at which point a shivering white-cheeked young girl hurries across the frozen square with her apron pulled over her face to avoid being frostbitten. She is, he notes, without color or colored glasses. A brutal reality surrounds her constantly. Her face is "pale with work and blue with cold; an eye supernatural with unrelated misery" (276).

Later, as he is touring the factory and learns that some of the rags used in paper making come from London, he wonders if any were "gathered from the dormitories of the Paradise of Bachelors." (280) An echo of the Temple is heard as he learns that the man who owns and runs the paper factory is a "bachelor" who wears gold buttons (284). As the narrator peers at the finished blank paper, he thinks of all the writing that will appear on these sheets, including lawyers' briefs and bills of divorce, like those that the bachelors spend their days writing. What goes unspoken is the fiction and poetry that Melville, himself, will write on these blank pages. Finally, on his return home, going out at Black Notch, he thinks of Temple Bar, and the last line is "Oh Paradise of Bachelors! And oh! Tartarus of Maids!" (286) With these references, Melville keeps his readers from forgetting the contrast between the world of the owners and the world of the owned.

LIVING CONDITIONS IN HELL

After his descent into the valley and before he enters the factory, the narrator has a brief glance of the workers' living conditions, which are in striking contrast to those of the Temple bachelors. Instead of the flower- and tree-lined lanes, the maids, like the workers in *Hard Times*, run in the cold through "irregular squares and courts," "a clustering of buildings" caused by the "broken, rocky nature of the ground." "Several narrow lanes and alleys, too, partly blocked with snow fallen from the roof, cut up the hamlet in all directions" (274).

He does not get inside the boardinghouses that surround the factory, but he does note their grim appearance from the outside and gets a glimpse of the interior when he knocks on a door for directions to the horse barn. A pale, shivering girl answers. That she is also described as "blue" suggests that the living quarters of these women are inadequately heated in this bitter cold.

INSIDE THE MILL

No work of fiction in the nineteenth century is so revealing of what goes on inside a factory as is Melville's "Tartarus of Maids." Realistic detail, joined with metaphor, underscores the dangers and humiliations with which the workers contended. The supremacy of the machine is emphasized as, in his approach to the factory, he notes a tower atop the central entryway. It reminds him of the tower over an ancient church in Temple Bar. Here, however, the tower is over a factory, confirming a grim reality: The church of the industrial revolution is not a place of worship but a factory.

In the first room he enters, the folding room, women fold the paper into envelopes and rule and stamp paper. What impresses him is the unbearable, mechanical monotony of the work. Of the workers doing the folding he writes, "At rows of blank-looking counters sat rows of blank looking girls, with blank, white folders in their blank hands, all blankly folding blank paper" (277). The monotony of the job itself seems to have seeped into, infected, the very character of the workers themselves. They have become little more than machine-like extensions of the main machine.

The first machine he sees is what he describes as a "huge iron animal," a term he will use repeatedly. It appears to dominate the pale worker sitting beneath it. She constantly "feeds" this insatiable animal with rose-tinted paper. Its piston unfailingly rises and falls, ironically stamping the paper with a tiny wreath of pink roses. His silent action of looking from the pink roses to the pallid cheeks suggests an ominous connection: The use of dyes to tint and stamp the paper was, at this time, unregulated, and it had the effect of poisoning the workers, resulting in their "pallid" cheeks. This stage of the paper-making process is rendered ironic because the rosy paper and stamp suggest a polite, genteel life that is far beyond the reach of these miserable workers. They are leached of health in order to provide the privileged class with pink roses.

The second machine, at which two young women work, puts lines on the blank foolscap. Again, the mindless monotony of the job, relieved briefly as they switch places, seems to have imprinted itself on their very souls, as we see that one of the women has a forehead lined to match the lined paper. A third machine, also referred to as an "iron animal," is on a high platform where it is waited on by two women, one in a dangerous position seated before it on a high stool, reminding the reader of the many workers who suffered death or maiming when they fell into machinery.

The arrogant Cupid, a young boy who serves as the narrator's guide, like Virgil to Dante, takes him on a tour of the remaining rooms in the factory, the first of which is the waterwheel room. His entrance into the room is further proof that this is a health-threatening environment for the workers. It is a damp, cold place where water from the Blood River pours over the power wheel. The foamy consistency and red color of the river suggests that it has been polluted at a source farther up and affects the health of the women who are in close quarters with it on a daily basis. It strikes the narrator that "red waters ... turn out white" cheeks (279).

The wet and rickety stairs lead to an upper room, called the rag room, which is divided into numerous stalls. One worker is assigned to each stall, "like so many mares haltered to the rack" (279). From the floor of each stall, a tall sword-like scythe is attached, and the girls rub bleached rags against it for the purpose of rendering them into the smallest of pieces, almost the size of lint, from which the paper will be made. Both Cupid and the narrator begin coughing from breathing in the lint. Of the scene, the narrator writes: "The air swam with the fine, poisonous particles, which from all sides darted, subtilely [sic], as motes in sunbeams, into the lungs" (279). Realizing the grave danger that breathing lint, day in and day out, presents to the workers, the narrator finds a sad irony in their sharpening the swords before them that produced the lint that has made them consumptive:

> So, through consumptive pallors of this blank, raggy life, go these white girls to their death (280).
>
> ...
>
> That moment two of the girls, dropping their rags, plied each a whet-stone up and down the sword-blade. My unaccustomed blood curdled at the sharp shriek of the tormented steel.
>
> Their own executioners: themselves whetting the very swords that slay them. (281)

Another unspoken peril lies in this process—this "raggy life"—revealed when the narrator asks, "Where do you get such hosts of rags?" and Cupid answers, "Some from the country round about; some from far over the sea—Leghorn and London." In 1850, only one year before Melville's visit to the Red Mill near his home in Pittsfield, the British author, Charles Kingsley, had published a widely read pamphlet called "Cheap Clothes and Nasty," detailing the contamination of cloth used in tailoring shops in London. Unspeakably filthy and infected with diseases of many kinds, the clothes made from this cloth infected the homes of the middle and upper classes that purchased it. Kingsley's popular novel titled *Alton Locke* was also published in 1850. In this work, a man dies after purchasing a new coat that had been made from material used to cover the bodies of three men dead of typhus fever. This was already a well-known problem first laid out in print as early as 1844, when English tailors themselves brought the matter to the attention of the public in a report. Melville does not show the reader the stage involving the unpacking of the heaps of rags and getting them into vats for bleaching, but his reference to the origin of many of the rags—from London—raises the issue of the rags' contamination.

The next room contains two large vats filled with a bubbling, gooey substance called pulp that will be fed into the machine in a farther room. Certain chemicals have been added to the rags, rendered into lint, to give them a glutinous consistency, like the white of an egg. As it boils, it stands to reason that it releases fumes into the air.

In a room beyond lies the monstrous, $12,000 paper-making machine that consists of numerous rollers, wheels, and cylinders. The pulp is poured into a channel to the machine and, for nine minutes, oozes along the long machine, under and over cylinders and rollers, looking more and more like the consistency of paper, until it drops in moist sheets at the end. An old woman, a former nurse who could no longer find work elsewhere, collects and stacks them. The whole inevitable process, in which the machine never breaks the delicate paper, is described as if it is a period of gestation.

It is here, at the end of the process of paper making, that the narrator experiences an epiphany about the machine so horrible that it leaves him physically faint:

> Something of awe now stole over me, as I gazed upon this inflexible iron animal. Always, more or less, machinery of this ponderous, elaborate sort strikes, in some moods, strange dread into the human heart, as some living, panting Behemoth might. But what made the thing I saw so specially terrible to me was the metallic necessity, the unbudging fatality which governed it. Though, here and there, I could not follow the thin, gauzy vail [sic] of pulp in the course of its more mysterious or entirely invisible advance, yet it was indubitable that, at those points where it eluded me, it still marched on in unvarying docility to the autocratic cunning of the machine. A fascination fastened on me. I stood spell-bound and wandering in my

soul. Before my eyes—there, passing in slow procession along the wheeling cylinders, I seemed to see glued to the pallid incipience of the pulp, the yet more pallid faces of all the pallid girls I had eyed that heavy day. Slowly, mournfully, beseechingly, yet unresistingly, they gleamed along, their agony dimly outlined on the imperfect paper, like the print of the tormented face on the handkerchief of Saint Veronica. (285)

Back in the folding room, the narrator learns particulars about the women he has just observed at their work. The bachelor owner tells him that they get few visitors in the isolated spot and that most of the girls come from distant villages to find work here. He also informs the narrator that the women work "twelve hours a day, day after day, through the three hundred and sixty-five days, excepting Sundays, Thanksgiving and Fast-days. That's our rule" (286). That would be the equivalent of working from six in the morning until six at night for six days a week.

THE FEMALE WORKER

The narrator gets a sense of how the workers are demeaned and debased when he realizes that all of them, even the older ones, are without exception called girls, instead of women. As he looks around the folding room after his tour of the machines, he asks, "Why is it, sir, that in most factories, female operatives, of whatever age, are indiscriminately called girls, never women?" The inadequate explanation the owner gives is that they are all unmarried, because he will not hire married women. So, whereas the bachelors relinquish their human nature by choice, the human nature of the maids is taken from them in their need to eke out a bare survival. To call the women, working in the New England factory, "girls" is a term of abasement similar to that dictated by the Southern plantation system where all grown black men were called "boys." Indeed, workers in northern factories in the United States were often called factory slaves. Melville's reference to their being called girls summarizes what he has witnessed in the factory: the cruelty and gross inequalities suffered by women, who were the primary workers in early textile, paper, and match-making factories, compared with men who, like the lawyers, are afforded education, professional standing, and a life of ease, and who, like Cupid and the paper mill owner, exploit and dominate the women.

As critic E.H. Eby concludes in his article in *Modern Language Quarterly*:

> The evidence which I have presented can lead to no other conclusion than that Melville constructed out of experiences and scenes around Pittsfield a story in which he presents the biological and social burdens of women contrasted with men. (100)

Critic Marvin Fisher, in a similar vein, in *Going Under*, writes that Melville's story is about "submissive and suffering femininity and aggressive impersonal force" (73).

THE MACHINE

The rise of the machine and the factory disturbs and counteracts Nature and the old life lived and dictated by Nature before the Industrial Revolution occurred. The narrator sees one hint of the old life on his way down the mountain when he glimpses a broken-down saw mill that might have flourished in the now faded agrarian culture—a mill that the owner may have operated himself. Now it is a ruin not far from the machines that have caused its demise.

The narrator refers to each machine as an iron animal that must be fed by the workers. Though the machines are inorganic, inert, lifeless pieces of iron, they have become gods. Note that none of the women can actually be said to *operate* the machines but merely to feed them and gather what they produce:

> Not a syllable was breathed. Nothing was heard but the low, steady overruling hum of the iron animals. The human voice was banished from the spot. Machinery—the vaunted [or praised] slave of humanity—here stood menially served by human beings, who served mutely and cringingly as the slave serves the Sultan. The girls did not so much seem accessory wheels to the general machinery as mere cogs to the wheels. (278)

Marvin Fisher, in *Going Under*, says Melville's aim in "Tartarus of Maids" was to express imaginatively the emotional impact of what he felt to be a general crisis for humanity: the widespread existence of a mechanical, life-deadening, freedom-denying set of values emphasized in America by increasing industrialization (p. 75).

What horrifies the narrator about the machines is their power over the workers, their deadening, unvarying monotony, their "metallic necessity" and inevitability, their "unbudging fatality" (284). The machines are life-less monsters that crush the life from the workers. Melville's depiction of the machine reminds the reader of the whale, Moby Dick: all powerful, destructive, unstoppable, but mindless, heartless, and meaningless.

In pondering what the machine is and what it represents, the narrator appears to be on the point of fainting—feeling chill in this hot room—and Cupid rushes him outside.

CUPID AND THE PERVERSION OF LOVE

A young boy named Cupid serves as his guide throughout the factory. He has the personality of the mischievous, brazen prankster of myth whose most famous hijinks are more damaging than compassionate. (See his part in the stories of Apollo and Daphne, and Demeter and Proserpine.) The narrator has a distinctly negative first impression of Cupid's arrogant, ill-mannered behavior toward the women workers. Something in Cupid's attitude suggests the widespread sexual abuse of women workers on the part of their supervisors which was documented in the early twentieth century. This is his first impression of the boy who hangs around but does not do any work:

> 'Cupid!' and by this odd fancy-name calling a dimpled, red-cheeked, spirited-looking, forward little fellow, who was rather impudently, I thought, gliding about among the passive-looking girls ... yet doing nothing that I could see. (278)

The words the narrator associates with Cupid are scarcely flattering, especially in this place where the factory system keeps its workers in the land of the dead. Cupid has an air of "boyishly-brisk importance" (278), which he displays throughout the tour as, for example, in the machine room when he answers the narrator's question with "a superior and patronizing air" (282). He ignores the fatal effect of the flying lint in the rag room that "stifles" the narrator and causes both of them to cough: the girls, he says dismissively, are used to it.

In one sense, the name *Cupid* is used ironically, in that Cupid, as he is popularly perceived, is associated with love. Yet this Cupid is himself without love or compassion. When the narrator asks Cupid why the workers are so sheet white, he answers with a heartless joke:

"'Why'—with a roguish twinkle, pure ignorant drollery, not knowing heartlessness—'I suppose the handling of such white bits of sheets all the time makes them so sheety'" (281). This confirms the narrator's bad impression of the young boy:

> More tragical and more inscrutably mysterious than any mystic sight, human or machine, throughout the factory, was the strange innocence of cruel-heartedness in this usage-hardened boy. (281)

Moreover, not only does Cupid himself lack charity or compassion, the factory, of which Cupid is a part, insists that these workers, in order to barely subsist, must relinquish the love they would find in being married and having children.

WHITENESS

References to death and hell pervade the sketch, and the main concepts that embody death and hell are whiteness, paleness, blankness, not unlike that of the white whale, Moby Dick. On his way to buy paper, the narrator is surrounded with the dazzling, icy whiteness of the frozen snow, more treacherous than beautiful. The ice causes his horse to plunge down the mountain and almost crash into a boulder, and it threatens the narrator with frostbite. The mountains around him look like white shrouds, and the whitewashed factory tucked into the snowy landscape at the bottom of the mountain blinds him. He cannot at first find the factory. As he enters, a blinding white light, reflected off the white snow, floods, "intolerably" through the huge windows.

In Western culture, white is traditionally associated with purity, like the white wedding gown of a bride. But whiteness here is mindlessness, sterility, and, as in other writings of Melville, like Moby Dick, cosmic horror and emptiness. As Captain Ahab suspects, maybe there is nothing—no meaning and no purpose—beyond the white façade of brutal nature. On a social as well as cosmic level, the same is true in "The Paradise of Maids." These workers live in a white world made meaningless for them by the machine. They suffer in the white world of nature that brings them nothing but bitter icy misery. And beneath that whiteness is nothingness and no redeeming purpose. The same is true of their workplace and work. The blank or lined white paper they produce has no meaning for them.

Like the mindless and destructive Moby Dick, the bleach and white lint are death-bringers, rendering the girls pale-cheeked—without meaningful purpose in lives dominated by the machine. Whiteness projects, magnifies, and validates a grim existential concept: The workers here suffer for no reason, either temporal or eternal.

As William Dillingham argues in *Melville's Short Fiction*, Tartarus and Paradise here are the same in some essential way: They are two worlds drained of life.

THE ISSUES IN THE TWENTIETH CENTURY

To escape the problem of union organizing, first begun by the Lowell workers, in the early decades of the twentieth century, owners began moving mills south, where labor was cheaper and unions were not part of the culture. The owners secured their profits and ease of operation, but the workers achieved nothing. In the first two decades of the century they were overworked, underpaid, and exposed to treacherous machines and killing humidity and lint, just as in the old days. Moreover, the practice of hiring children continued. Yet the southern way of paternalism and conservatism made unions unthinkable. Finally, workers had some hope for improvement in the administration of Franklin Delano Roosevelt when legislation was passed to limit work hours. But, instead of improving the lot of factory workers, it worsened it. Owners, now limited in the number of hours they could work their employees, instigated what was called "the speed-up," whereby the pace in front of the machines was accelerated.

QUESTIONS AND PROJECTS

1. Write an essay on Melville's presentation of the inequities in men's and women's work.
2. Conduct research on England's "Hungry Forties" and present a paper on it.
3. Write a paper contrasting the two portraits in Melville's "Poor Man's Pudding and Rich Man's Crumbs." Discuss the connection between this short story and the work at hand.
4. Have a discussion on why Melville's lawyers and the paper factory owner are all bachelors. In short, why did the author make this choice?
5. Have a class discussion on the Lowell mills, based on reports of various writings in the *Lowell Offering*.

6. Get a map of Massachusetts and circle the following: Melville's home of Pittsfield, Fall River, Lowell, South Hadley, Holyoke, Waltham, and Dalton.
7. Follow the map project with an investigation into the nineteenth-century industry in one of the locations.
8. Read and do an extensive oral report on William Moran's *Belles of New England*. Does his research enlarge our understanding of Melville's work?

FURTHER READING

Abbott, Edith. *Women in Industry*. New York; London: D. Appleton and Co., 1910.,

Baxandall, Rosalyn and Linda Gordon, eds. *America's Working Women*. W. W. Norton, 1995.

Berthoff, Warner, ed. *Great Short Works of Herman Melville*. New York: Harper and Row, 1969.

Campbell, Helen. *Women Wage Earners*. Boston: Robert Bros., 1893.

Cole, G.D.H. and Raymond Postgate. *The Common People:1746–1946*. London: Methuen, 1946.

Ringrose, Hyacinthe. *The Inns of Court*. Littleton, CO: F.B. Rothman, 1983.

Dillingham, William B. *Melville's Short Fiction*. Athens, GA: University of Georgia Press, 1977.

Dublin, Thomas. *Farm to Factory: Women's Letters, 1830–1860*. New York: Columbia University Press, 1981.

———. *Transforming Women's Work: New England Lives in the Industrial Revolution*. Ithaca, NY: Cornell University Press, 1994.

Eby, E. H. "Melville's 'Tartarus of Maids.'" *Modern Language Quarterly* 1 (1940):95–100.

Eisler, Benita, ed., *The Lowell Offering: Writings of New England Mill Women*. Philadelphia: J. B. Lippincott, 1977.

Fisher, Marvin. *Going Under: Melville's Short Fiction and the American 1850's*. Baton Rouge, LA: Louisiana State University Press, 1977.

Fogel, Richard Harter. *Melville's Shorter Tales*. Norman, OK: University of Oklahoma Press, 1960.

Foner, Philip S. *The Factory Girls*. Urbana, IL: University of Illinois Press, 1977.

Horsford, Howard C. "Melville in the Streets of London," Paper presented at the "Melville's Europe and American" session of the Modern

Language Association Convention, New York City, December 28, 1983.

Lerner, Gerda. "The Lady and the Mill Girl," *Midcontinent American Studies*, 1 (1969): 5–15.

MacClean, Annie Marion. *Wage Earning Women*. New York: Macmillan, 1910.

Moran, William. *The Belles of New England: The Women of the Textile Mills and the Families whose Wealth They Wove*. New York: St. Martin's Press, 2002.

Newman, Lea Bertani Vozar. *A Reader's Guide to the Short Stories of Herman Melville*. Boston: G.K. Hall, 1986.

Wertheimer, Barbara Mayer. *We Were There: The Story of Working Women in America*. New York: Pantheon, 1977.

4

Rebecca Harding Davis's
Life in the Iron Mills

In 1861, a Civil War began that would challenge the flourishing institution of black slavery. In that same year, just before the war began, a young woman named Rebecca Harding (the "Davis" would be added a decade later when she first married) saw into print an exposé of another kind of, not literal, but virtual slavery—the bonded labor of immigrant ironworkers in the industrial town of Wheeling where she lived. Wheeling, now a city in West Virginia was, at that time, in the slave border state of Virginia. *Life in the Iron Mills*, published by the prestigious *Atlantic* magazine, was an instant success. Nathaniel Hawthorne got in touch with Rebecca Harding and asked if he could come visit her in Virginia. He also invited her to Concord as his guest where she would have a literary coming-out party. She was feted on the same trip in Boston as a new literary star.

Davis's short story, sometimes regarded as the beginning of American realism, touches on a wide array of issues, both in the workplace and deriving from the workplace—conditions that, in slightly different degrees and forms, plague workers in the twentieth and twenty-first centuries. There are the matters of the exploitation of immigrant laborers, killing work, unreasonably long hours, low wages, starvation, toxic fumes that damage the workers and the communities, the escape into alcoholism, spiritual poverty, and thwarted rights to a full, healthy, and decent life. *Life in the Iron Mills* also raises the question of the damaging attitudes of both owners and reformers.

THE NARRATION

The story of Welsh immigrants performing hard labor in an industrial southern town is told by a sympathetic narrator, obviously a member of the educated class, who begins the tale while looking from the window of a house where immigrant workers once lived. After describing the stifling smog-filled atmosphere through which the sun cannot shine and the hopeless, sick mill workers walking by to and from work, she zooms in on one worker named Hugh Wolfe, an iron mill worker, and his cousin Deborah, a cotton mill worker who is in love with Hugh.

The story begins on one evening at about 11 P.M. as some of the female cotton mill workers have just gotten off and anticipate spending the rest of the evening losing themselves in drink at one of the bars. They are unable to persuade their fellow worker, Deborah, to join them. Instead she enters a house where six families live. Deborah, her cousin Hugh, and Hugh's father live in two basement rooms. Here Deborah finds Hugh's father collapsed on a bed of straw and a frail and starving young Irish girl, Janey, seeking shelter in the Wolfe quarters to avoid being left alone while her father is in jail.

Hearing that her cousin Hugh will be working until midnight, Deborah hastily packs what food she can find to take to him for his supper. Hugh and his mates are at work "rolling iron" in the manufacture of iron rails for train tracks. Hugh also, in his rest periods, sculpts figures out of korl, the refuse from the iron-making process.

On this night, as the men work and Deborah sleeps as she waits for Hugh to complete his shift, a group of distinguished gentlemen visit the mill: Kirby, the son of the owner; Clarke, an overseer; Dr. May, a local physician; a newspaper reporter; and Mitchell, Kirby's cynical brother-in-law. The visitors, staying in the mill to keep out of the rain, discover Hugh's sculpture of a desperate, hungry woman. They begin to argue about the social problems touching the workers.

For Wolfe, the appearance and sound of these elegant men constitute an epiphany. He is desperate in his hope to escape, desperate in his need for beauty. He takes seriously the doctor's words that he has a right to a life as free and beautiful as that of these men, a right to justice. He is also struck by Mitchell's words that all life comes down to money.

After Hugh and Deborah's return to their basement quarters, she gives him a green wallet that she has picked from Mitchell's pocket. It contains gold pieces and a check for an enormous amount of money. She tells him to use it to escape. Hugh grapples with the problem of whether to keep or return the money, and he goes briefly into church for guidance, exiting when he realizes that neither the congregation nor the minister has any understanding of the situation faced by him and his fellow workers. May's words that Hugh has a right to a better life and Mitchell's words, that money is the key, echo in his brain until Hugh decides to keep the money as a way of securing the life he has a right to live.

Hugh is arrested, of course, and tried and sentenced to 19 years in prison, partly as an example to the other workers. Deborah, being held in the cell next to his, is sentenced to 3 years. Hugh makes two frantic attempts to escape. Then, with a piece of tin honed to sharpness, he cuts himself and bleeds to death.

After Deborah's three years in prison, she is taken by a Quaker woman into the countryside to live where Hugh has been buried.

The story ends with the narrator, who turns to the curtain-covered korl sculpture in her house. At this moment, its arm extends outside the curtain, pointing its finger at a spot beyond the window, toward the East, where a new dawn will rise.

HISTORICAL BACKGROUND

By 1861, when *Life in the Iron Mills* was published, Wheeling, the town it describes, had been for many years a bustling industrial area because of its valuable natural resources and location. Situated on the Ohio River, it had an abundance of iron, coal, and white sand for the manufacture of glass and iron products. Mining iron ore had been well established by the turn of the nineteenth century, but the American iron industry clung to old methods of working iron. Not until 1816 was the first rolling mill, of the kind in which Hugh worked, built in the United States.

Wheeling's position as a transportation hub was enhanced with its connection to the 142-mile National Road in the early nineteenth century and, later, in the late 1840s, the bringing of the Baltimore and Ohio railroad into town. After the War of 1812, industry ballooned in Wheeling. Its most famous early mill, established in 1832 as Old Top Mill, made nails from the area's iron, and Wheeling was given the nickname "Nail City."

Other ironworks sprang up in the 1840s and 50s. Chief among them were rolling mills for refining pig iron in large vats over fires to produce the iron for products like rails. Numerous blast furnaces were built near the mines and near towns to prepare pig iron for the rolling mills. By 1860, Wheeling had the third largest number of rolling iron mills in the

United States. The larger mills in Wheeling included Benwood, LaBelle, Washington, Crescent, and Belmont rolling mills, the Flint Glass Works, the Riverside Spike Works, the Riverside Nail Works, a second glass works, a foundry, and Top Mill. In 1860, its other industrial assets that enhanced production included the smaller Hempfield Railroad, a waterworks, a bridge built for the Baltimore and Ohio Railroad across the Ohio River into Wheeling, and a steamboat landing.

The rolling mills had a consistent design. They were 100 × 300 feet rectangles with roofs but open on all sides. At one side were located the puddling and heating furnaces. Puddling was done by heating great iron vats to enormous temperatures, high enough to melt pig iron and burn off impurities. The puddler, like Hugh, stirred 300 pounds of molten pig iron for about a half an hour until it became balls of refined iron. These balls were extracted and placed on metal rollers to flatten them into sheets of iron or specific shapes like train rails. In nail factories, the iron was shaped into small strips and cut into nails. Puddling was the most physically arduous of all work with iron. Puddlers suffered heatstroke, exhaustion, and intense muscle strains, deterioration of their eyes, and tears in their skin caused by dry heat.

By midcentury the pollution from the coal burning in the glass and iron mills was horrendous. Sulfurous fumes deteriorated the lungs of the workers and permeated the air for miles around. Coal soot hung on trees and buildings and darkened the windows. Waste from slaughterhouses, soap and tallow makers, gasworks, oil refineries, mills, and sewers poured into Wheeling Creek. In the daytime, the sun was scarcely visible, and at night one never saw the stars. James E. Reeves, writing about the physical and medical topography of the city of Wheeling in 1870, described the industrial pollution there and the effect it had on both workers and residents:

Grass grows with difficulty in Wheeling, and many of the green yards in front of the houses are the result of much care. Neither do tender plants live in summer without constant washing; the leaves become coated with soot, the stomata choked, and respiration ceases. Indeed, Wheeling has acquired almost as much fame for its coal smoke and soot as for its mud, fogs, and manufactures. With every breath, the sooty particles enter the lungs and discolor the bronchial secretions; and housekeepers in the vicinity of the foundries, mills, and similar establishments are compelled to keep their windows continuously closed to keep out the soot. Some of the furnaces are positive nuisances from the quantities of carbon they emit as smoke. (quoted in Knowles 18)

Most workers lost their youth after a few years in the mills and most, by the age of 50 years, were dead of respiratory diseases, lung inflammation, chronic pneumonia, or consumption from breathing in poisonous fumes and mineral particles.

Immigrants from all over Europe and the British Isles came to the United States for work in the nineteenth century, chiefly in West Virginia, from Germany, England, Wales, Ireland, Scotland, Cornwall, and France. The Germans, usually artisans and businesspeople, constituted a third of the workforce in Wheeling. The French and Belgians worked as skilled artisans in the glass industry. Southern and Eastern Europeans worked in the coal mines, as did the Cornish. Irishmen worked on the railroads and the Welsh, like Hugh and his father, typically worked in the rolling iron mills. In the 1860 Wheeling census, 23 Welshmen worked in the city, and 23 of them were puddlers or puddlers' helpers. Although Irish women predominated in the cotton mills, women of all other nationalities worked there as well.

Though technically slave territory, the western part of what was then Virginia had a miniscule black population—less than 1 percent—and more free blacks than slaves. In this sense, Wheeling was more Midwestern than Southern.

The subject of labor strikes and demands arises in *Life in the Iron Mills* when Mitchell declares that once you tell the workers of their rights, they will strike for higher wages. One of the first important protests against working conditions in the coal and iron industry on the part of labor was a general strike in 1835 in Philadelphia, which was joined by coal heavers. Their demand was for a 10-hour day. In this early two-year period in the history of the United States (1835, 1836), there were 140 strikes throughout the eastern part of the country. It was not until the 1850s that puddlers, specifically, began organizing, first in the city of Pittsburgh. The iron molders of Philadelphia also established a union in that decade, protesting 14-hour shifts, speed-ups, and poverty-level wages. In 1861, the average wage for ironworkers rose to $12 a week. In 1863, strikes broke out in every industrial area, in every trade. In 1866, the ruling Iron Founders Association tried to lock out all members of the Molders Union. Puddlers in Wheeling made attempts at organizing in the 1860s, but it was not until six years after the publication of Davis's novel that they were able to establish two unions in Wheeling, called the Sons of Vulcan.

But the principal labor unrest in and around Wheeling before the Civil War, which thwarted the efforts to unite labor, was the violent hatred and competition between the workers themselves. In 1860 a political riot broke out between pro- and anti-Lincoln factions when Wheeling's large German population marched in support of Lincoln through the streets and were attacked by hard laborers from other countries. But animosity was not confined to that between workers from different countries. Those from a certain area of one country despised those from another area of the same country. Throughout the 1840s and 1850s in the Wheeling area, there were constant fights between railroad workers from different parts of Ireland for control of the work. Men were beaten up, shacks were burned, and large groups of workers were driven out entirely. Although the focus of the struggle was between two groups of workers, the unquestioned supremacy of one group over the other was regarded as an unspoken threat to the owners themselves, for the struggle illustrated what the workers could accomplish if they set their minds to it. In a real sense it prepared the workers for the larger struggle against the owners for decent hours and wages and safe work conditions, struggles that escalated during and after the Civil War.

MONEY AND THE MACHINE IN
LIFE IN THE IRON MILLS

The mill town of Davis's fiction is one in which money's supremacy—over talent, intelligence, religion, and compassion—had provided a few people with beauty, grace, and comfort. When the gentlemen make a trip to the mill where Hugh works, he notices this with his artist's eye and yearns for the ease and beauty they enjoy. Money has allowed these visitors to remain clean, neat, and stylish in appearance, in contrast to the workers. It has provided them with educations and elegant speech (no matter that what they actually say is insulting and insensitive). Why do these few live felicitous lives and most others, who create the wealth for them, live in pain? It comes down, as Mitchell explains to him, to money. Hugh asks, "That is it? Money?" (38). And when the doctor, sympathetic with Hugh only up to a point, tells Huge he has a right to a better life, Hugh rationalizes that he has a right to keep the money Deborah has stolen from Mitchell because it will provide him with an escape from the mills. "God made this money.... He never made the difference between poor and rich" (47). When Hugh is sentenced, he says to the court that "the money was his by rights, and that all the world had gone wrong" (51).

The creation of money for the few depends on the omnipotence of the machine. As it was throughout every nation that had undergone an industrial revolution, so it was here: The machine became the tyrant that made money for the owners and took the health and life of the worker in the process. Every human action had to be subordinate to the needs of the machine, portrayed as a unchallengeable monster. The narrator describes "a vast machinery of system by which the bodies of workmen are governed, that goes on unceasingly from year to year" (19). Only on Sunday do the machines release their hold on the worker. "But as soon as the clock strikes midnight, the great furnaces break forth with renewed fury, the clamor begins with fresh, breathless vigor, the engines sob and shriek like 'gods in pain'" (19).

WORK IN THE IRON MILLS

Hugh's job is one of the most difficult and damaging of any ironwork. He is positioned at the puddling furnace near the end of the rolling mill building. His job, like that of other puddlers, is to stir the molten, 300-pound iron mass with a long metal pole. He "dug into the furnace of melting iron with his pole, dully thinking how many rails the lump would yield" (26). At midnight the puddlers take the 300-pound ball of refined metal out of the furnaces and rake up the ashes. Before they leave, they put more pig iron into the furnaces and cover them.

The issue of work hours per day had already been raised in Pittsburgh, Philadelphia, Lowell, and other cities. Often workers ended up working 14-hour days. Deborah works the standard 12 hours a day "at the spools" in a textile mill as a picker—one who operates a machine that pulls apart cotton fibers (19). Deborah and other operatives leave work to go home at 11 P.M. There is a clear suggestion that it was expected that a worker get certain tasks done within the allotted time. If not, the work days were longer. One of the cotton mill workers, Kit Small, is still at work in the mill, past 11 P.M. because she is always behind in her work, even though her friends try to help her catch up. As Deborah goes to the mill to take Hugh some food, she encounters others who have just gotten off work.

The puddlers' hours are equally long. Hugh has been at the iron mill much of the day and works until midnight.

WAGES AND LIVING CONDITIONS

The reader is not told precisely what the workers are paid; one can only generalize from their living conditions that the wages are poverty level and inadequate to live on. For instance, the three members of the Wolfe family must live in two squalid rooms in the cellar of a house that they share with five other families. All workers in the community are doomed to "incessant labor, sleeping in kennel-like rooms, eating rank pork and molasses" (15). The floors of their rooms are made of dirt, covered with a "green slimy moss" (16). Wolfe's father sleeps on a bed of straw. Some workers, having no rooms, sleep on the heaps of ashes in the mills themselves.

The workers in these mills are spoken of as continually starving, without sufficient wages to buy enough food, much less decent food. Deborah's supper is cold boiled potatoes and a glass of sour ale. At 11 P.M., she has not eaten since morning. The narrator explains that although the potatoes provide her with sufficient food for her supper, on most days she went hungry. Janey, the young girl who also lives in the cellar, is also starving. She "greedily seized" the potato Deborah gave her (18). Deborah concludes that Hugh has not eaten since morning, and takes him some bread, her own ale that has soured, and salt port that has begun to rot.

THE EFFECTS OF THE FACTORY SYSTEM: DRUNKENNESS, POLLUTION, AND PHYSICAL DAMAGE

In their hopelessness and pain, most of the workers escape into very cheap, "rot-gut" alcohol—"strychnine whiskey" (49), which is little more than poison. The narrator makes references to it repeatedly. Men who work all night drink in the bars all day. Deborah's women friends head for the bars at 11 P.M., as soon as they get off work. Some of them appear to be drunk already. In the mill, the young owner's son makes a nasty reference to the workers' drinking habits, and Hugh responds that whiskey is sometimes the only thing they have to look forward to. The prison warden assumes from Deb's sickly stumbling that she has somehow acquired alcohol in jail. And in Hugh's dying vision of the community, he sees the men and women of the mills as "drunken and bloated" (60).

Drunkenness is not the only result of the mills. The story opens with the curse of pollution that the multiple mills have inflicted on the town.

It impresses itself on every sense. The prevailing foul smells insult the nose. The eye sees nothing but smoke everywhere; nothing escapes the back, greasy soot from the chimneys. It defaces the wharves and boats on the Ohio River, itself made yellow by pollution. It clings to houses, trees, even the faces and hands of people, and the mules carrying pig iron to the mills. Inside, the mill's pollution sullies both nature and art—the figure of a tiny angel and a caged canary.

The mill workers who walk past the narrator's window, going to and from work, are black with soot and ashes:

> Masses of men, with dull, besotted faces bent to the ground, sharpened here and there by pain or cunning; skin and muscle and flesh begrimed with smoke and ashes; stooping all night over boiling caldrons of metal, laired by day in dens of drunkenness and infamy; breathing from infancy to death an air saturated with fog and grease and soot, vileness for soul and body. (12)

The heavy work, long hours, inadequate food, alcohol, and pollution have taken tolls on the workers. Deborah, who doesn't drink, has a "ghastly" complexion, blue lips, and watery eyes. She is in constant pain and knows that she is not the only one; she has seen many women die of hunger or consumption (16).

Janey, with whom Wolfe is in love, and who lives in the same basement as the Wolfes, is described as "haggard and sickly; her eyes were heavy with sleep and hunger" (17).

Hugh, a young man in years, has grown bent, old, sickly, and weak. "He had already lost the strength and instinct vigor of a man, his muscles were thin, his nerves weak, his face (a meek, woman's face) haggard, yellow with consumption" (24). In prison the guards find his bed soaked with the blood he has spit up from his lungs. He has, his guard says, a death cough.

REFORM

The men who visit Hugh's workplace on the night when Deborah steals Mitchell's wallet each have different ideas about how society should be shaped or improved. Philosophers, with their eyes on God and their own souls, rarely consider the problems of these workers. Other men of charity who observe life in the iron mills become hardened and give up on any possibility of helping them. The mill overseer, typical of management, talks only of profits and costs. The reporter is only interested in business statistics. The son of the mill owner insists he is not responsible for the bleak lives lived here and demeans them as "a desperate set" (27), speaking about them and in front of them as if they were dumb animals incapable of understanding what he is saying. Mitchell compares his brother-in-law Kirby to Pontius Pilate, who washes his hands of responsibility in the trial of Jesus. The doctor, with a reputation as a philanthropist, is all words and no action. He feels sympathy for Hugh and tells him that he has rights but must help himself. Only the cynical Mitchell sees through his friends' points of view. He is convinced, he says, that "Reform is born of need, not pity" (39).

THE IRON AND STEEL INDUSTRY

To appreciate the persistence of issues raised in the story of Hugh Wolfe, it is instructive to examine the subsequent development of the iron and steel industry in which he worked. The industry was transformed after the Civil War with the introduction, in the United States, of the Bessemer processing system and the Siemens-Martin open-hearth method of the Bessemer system. Although Henry Bessemer, an Englishman known as the father of the steel industry, had in 1855 patented his smelting system to make high-quality ingots more quickly and efficiently, the first Bessemer mill was not built in the United States until 1864. And the more efficient version of the open-hearth furnace was not built until 1868. Steel, which replaced most iron use, is a product, made of iron, that has greater strength, hardness, and elasticity than iron. After the Civil War, the steel industry grew by leaps and bounds under the ownership of industrial barons who had little concern for their workers. By 1910, the United States began producing more steel than any other country in the world. The industry grew consistently throughout the first six decades of the twentieth century, reaching its peak in 1969.

But in the 1960s, United States steel companies began to be bothered by serious competition from foreign countries that could produce steel more efficiently with cheaper labor. As a result, the industry went into decline. Whereas some 141,262,000 tons of steel were produced in the United States in 1969, by 1975 it had dropped to 89,000,000 tons. In the 1970s, steel mills began closing across the northeast and southeast, and communities based on the steel industry became ghost towns.

THE STRUGGLE OF IRON AND STEELWORKERS

The gentlemen who visit Hugh Wolfe's workplace are provoked to discuss the matter of reform by the squalor they see there. Kirby, the son of the owner, expresses his opinion that the men are dangerous. Mitchell brings up briefly the threat of the men striking for higher wages and, expresses his disgust at the workplace and the condition of the workers, says that "some day, out of their bitter need will be thrown up their own light-bringer,—their Jean Paul, their Cromwell, their Messiah" (39). And throughout the struggles of steel mill workers that followed the Civil War, leaders did arise from the ranks of workers, but even in the face of abominable conditions, iron- and steelworkers were not to realize decent working condition for more than seven decades after Hugh Wolfe listens to the discussion of the gentlemen in his workplace.

Toward the end of the nineteenth century, when the United States steel industry was growing into the largest in the world and its barons were multimillionaires, workers in the industry were still grossly underpaid, overworked, and physically at risk on the job. In July 1892, encouraged by the Amalgamated Association of Iron, Steel, and Tin Workers, laborers in Andrew Carnegie's Homestead Steel works in Pennsylvania struck and eventually took over the mills and town after Henry Clay Frick, manager of the mills, announced a nonnegotiable plan to cut wages. This was the point of desperation that Mitchell had spoken of, that provoked the workers to action. In response, Frick sent in 300 Pinkerton men to guard and run the mill. Clashes inevitably broke out, leaving several dead. The state militia was called in to protect the mills and nonunion workers from the strikers. Five months later it became obvious that the strike had failed. Many lost their jobs at Homestead and were no longer able to work anywhere in their trade. The failure of the Homestead strike also spelled the end of the emerging iron and steelworkers' union. It took 40 years for a lasting and effective union to appear again.

The second major upheaval on the part of iron and steelworkers came in 1919, after World War I. Wages were again the issue—wages so low that a livable standard of living was impossible. The cost of living had doubled since before the war, but wages had declined. The Interchurch World Movement Commission of Inquiry (quoted in Boyer and Morais 206) determined that a weekly wage for minimal survival was $38.92 a week, but miners were making from $26.90 to $29.98 a week, and steelworkers were making $34.19 a week. In light of expenses, these wages would leave the workers of 1919 in living conditions only slightly changed from 1861.

The same commission gave a graphic portrait of the workplace itself in 1919 to show the hard and dangerous work required of steelworkers, a picture that is not so far removed from the work Hugh Wolfe performed:

Job of the third helper, open hearth furnace: With other helpers he makes 'back wall' which means throwing heavy dolomite with a shovel across blazing furnaces to the back wall, to protect it for the next batch of hot steel. Heat above 180 degrees at the distance from which the shovelful is thrown in; each shoveler wears smoked goggles and protects his face with his arm as he throws. After a back wall, it is necessary to rest at least 15 minutes. A man may have 4 or 5 hours to himself out of the 14 hour shift or he may work hard the whole turn. He may have two or three easy days or he may have a week of the most continuous and exhausting toil.

The third helper fills large bays with coal to throw into a ladle at tap time; easy to burn your face off. Helps drill a 'bad' hole at tap time, work of the most exhausting kind; also must shovel dolomite into ladle of molten steel. This is the hottest job and certainly the most exposed to minor burns. Temperature around 180 degrees. Nearly every tap time leaves three or four small burns on neck, face, hands or legs....

On the blast furnaces. Job of the stove gang: Six to ten men in a gang keep the blast furnace stoves cleaned; as stove cools, gang cleans out hardened cinder in combustion chamber with pick and shovel. Men go inside the stove. Before going in the man puts on heavy wooden sandals, a jacket which fits the neck closely, and heavy cap with ear flaps; also goggles. Cleaning out the flue dust is not so hot, but men breathe dust-saturated air. Hardest job is 'poking her out,' ramming out the flue dust in checker work at top of stove. Large pieces of canvas tied over feet and legs to keep heat from coming up legs; two pairs of gloves needed, handkerchiefs cover all head except eyes. Three minutes to ten minutes at a turn are the limit for work in the chamber at the top of the stove; very hard to breathe. Hours: twelve hours a day. (quoted in Boyer and Morais 206, 207)

The workers grievances, in addition to starvation wages, included unreasonable hours, sometimes 24-hour shifts, seven days a week, no overtime pay, and hostility toward unions.

Four million workers in different trades struck in 1919, but the most momentous was the strike of steelworkers. Both owners and workers knew that the existence of labor unions in America depended on the success of strikes against the all-powerful steel industry. Strikes broke out in 50 cities in 10 states.

Steel mill owners, refusing to negotiate, stonewalled the strikers, enlisted government assistance, including the U.S. Army, veterans, paid spies and vigilantes, deputy sheriffs, and private detectives. In the course of the strike, 22 workers were killed, hundreds were wounded or beaten up, and several thousand were arrested. As they waited out the strike, 1.5 million workers starved. The strike failed miserably, and low wages, long hours, and dangerous workplace conditions continued with little challenge for almost two decades.

Not until the 1930s were steelworkers successfully organized. The suffering of all people, but particularly laborers, during the great economic depression of that time incited steelworkers to organize with a vengeance for decent wages and workplace conditions. By 1936, there were 5,000 volunteers who fanned out into steel mills in the United States and opened highly efficient, well-staffed offices in three large, key steel areas: Chicago, Birmingham, and Pittsburgh. By the end of 1937, after the automobile workers' great success in Flint, Michigan, the steelworkers union swelled to 150,000 members. Surprisingly, U.S. Steel, the largest of the steel companies, acceded, without a fight and the necessity of a strike, to the union workers' demands. The company agreed to a 10 percent increase in wages, a 40-hour week, and company recognition of the union.

But smaller steel companies, collectively called Little Steel, refused the union's demands and, according to the LaFollett congressional committee on labor, stockpiled machine guns, rifles, revolvers, tear gas, and bombs in anticipation of the strike. Seventeen workers died of gunshot wounds and beatings; 10 were critically wounded, and 150 were treated in hospitals for injuries. Nevertheless, in the 1940s, workers for Little Steel eventually won a 10 percent raise; a five-day, 40-hour week; and union recognition.

The power of unions and the size of its membership, including the AFL-CIO to which steelworkers belonged, were at their heights in the 1950s. And the sympathetic administrations of John Kennedy and Lyndon Johnson extended protection to working-class people.

However, several developments have worked to the detriment of iron and steelworkers since the 1970s. First was the shutting down of steel mills throughout the country, largely because of competition from abroad. As a result, thousands of laborers were thrown out of work.

At the same time, the power of unions to protect workers was undermined because of federal deregulation, which took power from the workers and gave it to the owners. This resulted in a rise in nonunion work and union concessions. The National Labor Relations Act began working to the detriment of workers. In President Ronald Reagan's administration, workers and unions suffered defeat after defeat. By 1985, union membership had declined by five million workers. Collective bargaining declined. Federal policies and national trends throughout the 1980s continued to make the lives of laborers more difficult. For instance, the living standard for workers began declining for the first time since the Great Depression.

In 2004 union membership fell to its lowest level in 60 years, down 300,000 in just one year. Much of the deterioration is attributable to industries' practice of outsourcing to countries with cheaper labor. Since 2001, there has been a loss of three million factory jobs. Another factor in the decline of unions is the government's persistent barriers thrown up to discourage workers from uniting to improve their economic situations. The government has also unapologetically supported owners who want to use every angle to discourage unions. The puzzle is that while membership in unions is declining, polls of workers show that around 50 percent of them want to be in unions.

TWENTY-FIRST-CENTURY WORKPLACE HAZARDS

Even as he took his own life, Hugh Wolfe was dying from work-induced lung disease, as were most of his fellow ironworkers and the textile workers and miners in the area of Wheeling. More than 100 years later, workers are still being maimed and dying from the work they do. And the chief work-related ailment is the same that afflicted Hugh: occupational lung disease. In 1998, 17,315 laborers died of lung cancer induced by pollutants they inhaled in the workplace.

Miners, construction and demolition workers, shipyard workers, installers of tile, electricians, pavers, brake-liners, maintenance workers, and many others who had worked with asbestos before it was found to be cancer causing in 1975 are still dying of lung cancer in the twenty-first century. Some trades bring workers in contact with asbestos installed in the early twentieth century, still putting them at risk for lung cancer in the twenty-first century.

Textile dusts, like those that poisoned Deborah and her fellow workers, are still a danger to the lungs of laborers. The disease, called brown lung, obstructs the lungs' small airways and kills or disables those who breathe hemp, flax, and cotton dust.

Coal dust, breathed by miners, causes the deadly black lung that killed 59,000 miners between 1968 and 1992. More than 1.6 million workers in mines, foundries, blasting, and stone, glass, and clay industries have been exposed to silica, which leads to a variety of lung impairments. Cancer-causing agents exist in any workplace that produces or uses chemicals in the process of manufacture.

The illnesses of immigrants and minority workers in the chicken-processing industry are twice the national average. Moreover, one in five is injured on the job. These workers inhale ammonia, salmonella, and other bacteria on the job. Often they cough up blood. They also suffer cuts and eye injuries from the fowl, and in working with knives under speed-ups, finger amputation is not uncommon.

INDUSTRIAL POLLUTION

In *Life in the Iron Mills*, the narrator writes at length of the soot that covers every surface, the green slime that creeps down walls, and the smog that covers the sun. This particular polluter of the atmosphere that comes from burning soft coal, for example, has long since been made illegal. In the 1970s, in fact, the United States was the world's leader in protecting the environment. But by 2004, the government had rewritten factory emissions guidelines to permit factories much more leeway than before in creating harmful emissions, leading to the resignation of the administration's director of the Environmental Protection Agency. Attempts to regulate vehicular emissions came to a standstill. And the administration refused to ratify the Kyoto accords, reached by nations across the globe to address the problem of global warming.

It is clear that the workplace issues of wages, hours, safety, pollution, and reform, which Rebecca Harding Davis raised in an early novel of the plight of the worker, are alive and pertinent in the twenty-first century.

QUESTIONS AND PROJECTS

1. Conduct some research on the present configuration of immigrants in the United States. What are the social problems regarding immigrants? What legislation is being proposed with reference to immigrants? Write your findings in the form of a report.

2. Into what jobs do immigrants go and why? Present this as a report to your class.
3. Have a debate on the current issues regarding immigrant workers in the United States.
4. Stage a mock trial of Hugh Wolfe, accused of stealing. Determine his guilt or innocence and his sentence if he is found guilty.
5. Conduct research on one industrial threat to the environment. Be prepared to have a class discussion on each problem.
6. Do research on strip mining in West Virginia in the twenty-first century.
7. Invite a speaker on the environment to your class. Be sure to plan for a question-and-answer period. Assign two students to take notes of this class period.
8. Invite a speaker from a local union to your class. Be sure to plan for a question-and-answer period. Assign two students to take notes of this class period.
9. Do research and write a paper on one of labor's leaders who has risen from the ranks of labor.
10. Find some early photographs of ironworkers—English or American—for class display.
11. Choose any year in the nineteenth century for which you can find data and list the weekly salary of any common laborer. Then figure out what he or she could buy with the salary by looking at the cost of housing and food in the same period.
12. Do the same research for a year in the twenty-first century.
13. What protections for workers were put into place in the administration of Franklin Roosevelt. Are those protections still in effect?

FURTHER READING

Boyer, Richard O. and Herbert M. Morais. *Labor's Untold Story.* New York: United Electrical, Radio and Machine Workers of America, 1955.

Davis, Rebecca Harding. *Life in the Iron Mills.* Ed. Tillie Olsen. Old Westbury, NY: The Feminist Press, 1972.

Fried, Albert. *Except to Walk Free.* Garden City, NY: Anchor Books, 1974.

Greenhouse, Steven. "Forced to Work Off the Clock. Some Fight Back," *New York Times.* Friday 19 November 2004: A1.

———. "Membership in Unions Drops Again." *New York Times.* 11 January 2005: A5.

Harris, Sharon M. *Rebecca Harding Davis and American Realism.* Philadelphia: University of Pennsylvania Press, 1991.

Jackson, Derrick Z. "Neglecting Mother Earth," *The Boston Globe.* Wednesday 26 January 2005: 18.

Lasseter, Janice Milner and Sharon M. Harris. *Rebecca Harding Davis.* Nashville, TN: Vanderbilt University Press, 2001.

Pfaelzer, Jean. *Parlor Radical.* Pittsburgh, PA: University of Pittsburgh Press, 1996.

Rose, Jane Atteridge. *Rebecca Harding Davis.* New York: Twayne Publishers, 1993.

Semple, Robert B., Jr. "Christie Whitman Rides to the Defense of Her Grand Old Party," *New York Times.* Tuesday 1 February 2005: A22.

Shipler, David K. *The Working Poor.* New York: Alfred A. Knopf, 2005.

Tichi Cecelia, "Introduction : Cultural and Historical Background." Rebecca Harding Davis. *Life in the Iron Mills.* Boston: Bedford/St. Martin's, 1998.

Zinn, Howard. *A People's History of the United States.* New York: HarperPerennial, 1980.

5

Herman Melville's "Bartleby, the Scrivener: A Story of Wall Street"

In 1853, two years before his sketch of the London Inns of Court, Herman Melville saw into print "Bartleby, the Scrivener: A Story of Wall Street," set in an American lawyer's workplace. Again, as he had done in his seafaring novels and would do in "The Paradise of Bachelors and the Tartarus of Maids," Melville provides the reader with one of the most realistic, explicit pictures of a nineteenth-century workplace. This time his focus is on the white-collar office worker—the scrivener or clerk. To this day, no fictional account of an office workplace can come close to the detail of "Bartleby, the Scrivener." The short story can be approached on a variety of levels: as a comment on the plight of the creative writer whom Bartleby represents; as a heartbreaking rendering of the pain and sorrow of the human condition in general; and as a specific examination of the dehumanization of workers in a capitalistic, which is to say money-driven, culture. The social issues Melville raises include the paying of poverty-level wages for long hours of work; the mindless monotony of the work that destroys individuals; the hopelessness that is bred by the impossibility of advancement from low-level clerical work; the physical and emotional problems that ensue from the psychological strain of work; and the materialistic system of values to which workers are sacrificed.

THE NARRATIVE

The narrator of "Bartleby, the Scrivener" is an elderly, successful Wall Street lawyer, whose office is the setting of the story. He first introduces himself—his considerable reputation, his connections with wealthy people like John Jacob Astor, and his capitalistic values.

Having established his own vision of himself, he turns to the subject of his employees—Turkey, his older copyist, who is alcoholic; his ambitious younger employee, Nippers, who suffers from digestive disorders; and Ginger Nut, his youthful intern, who now functions primarily as an errand boy. Not until nine pages into the story is the title character, Bartleby, his third copyist, introduced.

Bartleby's arrival is the plot's initiating circumstance, the event that disrupts the "snug" office, as the narrator sees it, for on his third day at work, Bartleby refuses to join in the work of correcting copy, with the words, "I would prefer not to." This is the most boring, most mindless part of the scrivener's job. Nothing the kindly but misguided narrator can do changes Bartleby's mind. The narrator, above all not wanting an unpleasant scene, thinks about but decides not to dismiss him. A few days later, Bartleby again refuses to join the others, this time in correcting his own copy. Each time he refuses and further refuses to do the smallest errand requested by the narrator.

The narrator, on his part, is thrown into an intellectual quandary by this irritant in his snug office. He tries to prod Bartleby to quit the job and leave, but when Bartleby refuses, the narrator, to keep tranquility in his office, resists creating a scene by forcibly having him removed. So, one (many would say the main) element of the plot is comprised of the narrator's internal crisis as he contemplates what to do about Bartleby and how to justify his own failure to act.

On a Sunday morning, the narrator drops by his office to discover that Bartleby has been actually living in the workplace. He comes to the conclusion that his strange employee is mentally unstable. He again considers dismissing Bartleby but, seeing the difficulty in doing that, decides not to. Meanwhile, Bartleby who has refused to do any work except copy, now also refuses to do even that, and the narrator is forced to give him six weeks' notice. But at the end of six weeks, Bartleby is still there and shows no sign of leaving.

Finally, the narrator rationalizes his own inaction and allows Bartleby to remain in the office, even though the copyist refuses to leave the building, even for a minute, and will not respond to any request or order to do work.

But there is finally something even more important to the narrator than maintaining peace in his office. When Bartleby's bizarre presence begins to draw the attention of the narrator's associates and clientele, threatening the success of his business, the narrator decides to rid himself of Bartleby—not by having the police force Bartleby out, but by moving out his whole business office and leaving Bartleby behind. But this doesn't work either. The new tenants in his old office hold him responsible for getting Bartleby out. Eventually, the police take Bartleby to jail, appropriately called "the Tombs." The narrator visits him there and tries to provide for him, but Bartleby refuses and dies in prison as passively as he has lived, by starving himself to death.

The tale concludes with the narrator's investigation into Bartleby's past. He has good reason to believe that Bartleby worked for a time in a federal "dead letter office," burning letters that could not be delivered. Like Bartleby and other human beings, the letters are conceived in hope, but are destroyed in the end.

THE CONTEXT

The rise of capitalism in nineteenth-century America is firmly in the historical background of Melville's tale. By the 1820s in the United States, technology and new means of efficiency had led to the rapid development, not only of factories, but of railroads and the exploitation of the nation's vast raw materials in the West. The promise of wealth in these arenas attracted entrepreneurs and investment in the East. Capital—that is the money or property used in investment—was needed to develop industry and transportation, and assumed tremendous actual and ideological importance. Money "worked," as did human operatives, only the work of money was now deemed more important. Thomas C. Cochran and William Miller graphically document the tenor of the business world as it was evolving in the first half of the century:

In the United States each year after 1800, more and more men spent their days in factories and mines, on canals and railroads, tending machines, locomotives, and steamboats, keeping accounts, selling commodities, digging coal, copper, lead, and iron, drilling oil and natural gas. As time passed they spent their profits, wages, and commissions on goods announced for sale in newspapers supported by business advertisements and friendly to business objectives. Their literature was issued by publishers engaged in business enterprises. Their amusements were not spontaneous street dances but spectacles staged for profit. Their colleges, founded in many areas to prepare young men for the ministry of God, became devoted to science, and their scientists became servants of business. Their public architecture concerned itself with banks, insurance offices, grand hotels for commercial travelers. Their mature philosophy discarded metaphysics—or so its practitioners claimed, describing their speculation felicitously for our pecuniary culture as the quest for "cash value" of ideas. (1)

In the 1830s, New York City, with goods pouring into and out of the port, fed by the Erie Canal, became the business capitol of the country, and business activity came to be centered on Wall Street in lower Manhattan. Through the stock market located there, men with money invested in promising new techniques and gathered in profits. In the two decades between 1837 and 1857, the government facilitated rampant, unchecked growth of businesses and monopolies, allowing them to run slipshod over workers and everything else in American society. Between 1851 and 1853, trading in stocks and bonds on Wall Street was exceptionally active as brokerage houses, credit businesses, law offices, and insurance companies burgeoned.

The new capitalists, in pursuit of the tremendous wealth that lay before them, had the full encouragement and cooperation of the United States government, but they reached their goals by ruthlessly putting down any competition, establishing monopolies, charging high prices, and paying low wages. (See Zinn 1995.)

At the time Melville wrote "Bartleby the Scrivener," lawyers on Wall Street, who managed huge holdings in stocks, bonds, and real estate, had the most lucrative businesses of any other professionals in the city. Historian Edward Pessen depicts the business situation as it existed in the 1840s and 1850s on Wall Street and the function of the lawyer/narrator who says he never enters a courtroom:

Even in the great cities, rich men usually classified as lawyers appear to have derived most of their wealth from fields other than law. During the second quarter of the nineteenth century, lawyer-capitalists may have been attorneys in terms of their identifiable occupations. As wealthholders, however, they were primarily merchants, investors, corporate officers, and real estate owners—in addition to being sons and sons-in-law to the rich. (58)

Wealth in the hands of a relatively few families generated a high demand for service personnel: salespersons, housekeepers, stewards, nurses, midwives, laundresses, barbers, and hairdressers. And, in the 1840s and 1850s, the constant movement of paper currency, stocks, bonds, and real estate created the demand for tens of thousands of office operatives: copyists, clerks, office boys, bookkeepers, accountants, and real estate and insurance agents. They worked in offices accurately described by Melville in "Bartleby." Note the similarities between the office of the narrator in "Bartleby" and Matthew Smith's 1869 description of the office of the son of John Jacob Astor, prominently mentioned in Melville's tale:

> On Prince Street, just out of Broadway, is a plain one-story build-ing, looking not unlike a country bank. The windows are guarded by heavy iron bars. Here Mr. Astor controls his immense estate. In 1846, Mr. Astor was reputed to be worth five millions. His Uncle Henry, a celebrated butcher in the Bowery, left him his accumu-lated wealth, reaching half a million. By fortunate investments, and donations from his father, he is now supposed to be worth forty millions. His property is mostly in real estate, and in valuable leases of property belonging to Trinity Church. At ten o'clock every morn-ing Mr. Astor enters his office. It consists of two rooms. The first is occupied by his clerks. His sons have a desk on either side of the room. In the rear room, separated from the front by folding doors, is Mr. Astor's office. (187)

A more dismal office is found in Charles Dickens's "A Christmas Carol," where Bob Cratchit works six days a week for "fifteen bob," scarcely as much as a U.S. dollar:

> The door of Scrooge's counting-house was open that he might keep his eye upon his clerk, who in a dismal little cell beyond, a sort of tank, was copying letters. Scrooge had a very small fire, but the clerk's fire was so very much smaller that it looked like one coal. But he couldn't replenish it, for Scrooge kept the coal-box in his own room; and so surely as the clerk came in with the shovel, the master predicted that it would be necessary for them to part. Wherefore the clerk put on his white comforter, and tried to warm himself at the candle; in which effort, not being a man of a strong imagination, he failed. (423–424)

There was a distinct class division between the clerks who worked in Wall Street offices. One group was considered to have the same social standing as their bosses. These were composed of the sons of wealthy men, young men who served brief apprenticeships as clerks in order to learn to be lawyers or businessmen. They left their clerkships in their early twenties to join the professional world, actually becoming colleagues on equal footing with their old bosses. Most of them were not and did not need to be paid. After work they returned to the comfortable houses of their well-off fathers and still had the money to pursue an interesting social life and stimulating entertainments. When historians speak of the grand opportunities for clerks to rise in the world, they are speaking of this class only.

The majority of clerks, however, were in a vastly different class. They were usually the sons of poor tradesmen or artisans who saw clerking as an escape from hard physical labor. They dressed and spoke as gentlemen and developed refined manners. Despite the accomplishments of clerks from poor backgrounds, there was a clear demarcation between them and their high-born colleagues, for whereas the latter were able to quit their clerical jobs and move up, the poorer class of clerks were doomed to support themselves from the outset and to remain as low-paying clerks for the rest of their lives.

Money made the difference. In one of the few accounts of nineteenth-century clerks, B. G. Orchard describes, in an 1871 survey, the finances in a Liverpool law office, similar to that of the narrator's:

> The Law, though in popular estimation respectable and mysteriously dreadful, is about the poorest grazing ground a clerk can feed on. Lawyers and law stationers do not need men of talent ...; for the work not done by the principals or the managing clerk is of the dreariest routine character, and incomes earned by the legal gentlemen being, on the average, smaller than those that reward the enterprising exertions of employers in other businesses, it is only natural for them to save all they can in office expenses. (35)

Because lawyers had a steady stream of interns who came to their office to learn a trade and, therefore, were unpaid, they had little demand for paid clerks. This allowed them to keep salaries low and to fire clerks whenever they wished.

THE FACE OF BUSINESS

The lawyer narrator, who is well-intentioned up to a point, is the epitome of the unbridled capitalism that dominated American society before and after the Civil War. In understanding him, we get a picture of how workers at the time suffered as just so many cogs in the wheels of big business. His values are the values of capitalism, to which the humanity of the workers is sacrificed. Consistent with the course of big business, even though he is a man of the law, his interest is in profits, not justice. His comments about what situations make him angry are telling. The narrator rarely loses his temper, "much more seldom indulge[s] in dangerous indignation at wrongs and outrages" (4). But he *had* almost lost his temper when a lucrative sinecure was denied him. So he is a lawyer who does not become indignant at wrongs and outrages—read "injustices."

He practices the kind of law that never requires him to enter a courtroom to fight for justice. Instead, he says he "does a snug business among rich men's bonds, and mortgages, and title deeds" (4). Later, he describes himself more specifically as a "conveyancer and title hunter, and drawerup of recondite documents of all sorts" (11).

People betray themselves in choosing their heroes. And the narrator reveals himself and his values in his enthusiastic admiration of John Jacob Astor, notorious as the most ruthless capitalist of his age, especially in his manner of handling real estate transactions in New York City. The narrator brags about the compliments Astor has paid him and about having been hired by Astor in the past. Moreover, the narrator loves to repeat the name of John Jacob Astor, because, he says, it sounds like gold.

The narrator's view of his employees is consistent with the stance of owners toward workers. He does not see them as men, but as Dickensian caricatures. He makes a joke of their foibles and suffering. He is disdainful of what he calls Turkey's insolence and compares him to a frisky horse, saying of Turkey's pride in the cast-off coat the narrator gives him, that Turkey felt his coat as a "restive horse is said to feel his oats. It made him insolent. He was a man whom prosperity [In the form of a cast-off coat] harmed" (9).

He also belittles and disapproves of Nippers' desire to improve himself, to have a better life for himself. Nippers is not content with his job as a copyist, and this behavior, in the narrator's eyes is symptomatic of "diseased ambition" (8).

The key to his profit-driven values, what really matters to him, can be traced through the references or allusions to charity throughout the tale. In the fashion of many businesspeople of his day, he performs acts of charity, not from a loving heart, but out of self-interest. He is not unlike a man who donates millions of dollars to a hospital chiefly because he needs a tax break and likes the idea of a hospital wing being named for him. The narrator gives Turkey his old coat, not because the old man is otherwise cold, dirty, and ragged, but because he finds Turkey's own coat to be an embarrassment that, he says, reflects poorly on his chambers.

He yields to Turkey's refusal to stay away from work in the afternoons, when he does more damage than work, not out of pity for an old man, but because he is afraid of the turbulence Turkey would cause over the matter in the office if he were ordered to stay away half a day. His motivation is always selfish, shown in his repeated phrase in speaking of one and another employee, "he is useful to me."

The case of Turkey foreshadows his dealing with Bartleby in which, again, he proves that true charity has no place in this business world. Although he is touched by Bartleby's plight, he continues to allow Bartleby to stay in his chambers, not so much because he pities him, but because he does not want a scene. But he must rationalize his weak inaction, and, in so doing, the argument always comes down to "me." He speaks of Bartleby (before he quits copying altogether) as "a valuable acquisition," a thing he has bought, not a person (20). When Bartleby then refuses to copy, the narrator summons up that word "charity" to justify his continued inaction, but undercuts his charity at every turn. It is not love freely given for the sake of someone else; it is love that is useful and of benefit to the giver:

> But when this old Adam of resentment rose in me and tempted me concerning Bartleby, I grappled with him and threw him. How? Why? Simply by recalling the divine injunction: 'A new commandment give I unto you, that ye love one another.' Yes, this it was that saved *me*. Aside from higher considerations, charity often operates as a vastly wise and prudent principle—a great safeguard to *its possessor*.... *Mere self interest,* then, if no better motive can be enlisted, should especially with high-tempered men, prompt all beings to charity and philanthropy. (34; emphasis added)

The businessman's reading in the theology of Joseph Priestley and Jonathan Edwards relieves him of all responsibility. Since, as they argue, everything is preordained by God, there is really nothing the narrator can really do to change his employee's situation.

Earlier, he had admitted that "up to a certain point the thought or sight of misery enlists our best affections; but, in certain special cases, beyond that point it does not" (24). Now a situation arises that forces the businessman to put his true values on the table. Bartleby attracts the unwanted attention and dismay of his clients and fellow attorneys, "scandalizing my personal reputation," therefore threatening his business. He acknowledges that he must now choose between his business and what the Bible he frequently quotes calls "one of the least of these" (a stand-in for Christ), and he chooses his business.

Finally, with Bartleby in the Tombs, the narrator asks him to come home with him, surely realizing that the offer comes too late.

THE OFFICE

To fully grasp the suffering of the clerks in "Bartleby, the Scrivener," it is imperative to understand the details of their surroundings and their day-to-day duties. The position of the narrator's law office on Wall Street emphasizes its function as a server of capitalism and money: "rich men's bonds, and mortgages, and title deeds" (4), And its physical appearance underscores the misery of the workers who sacrifice their lives in the service of Wall Street.

Other edifices in the neighborhood, near Canal and Broadway, include the Post Office, which is a three-minute walk away, various cheap eating houses that draw their customers from the ranks of ill-paid clerks, Trinity Church (a large landholding corporation attended by the very wealthy), City Hall, and the Hall of Justice, in which is located the Tombs, or prison.

The office is located on the second floor of a three-story building closely surrounded by taller structures. It is in an area of "densely populated law buildings." On the top floor lives a woman who cleans the office. At one end of the chambers, one looks on "the white wall of the interior of a spacious sky-light shaft," which he says, "is deficient in what landscape painters call 'life'" (4). At the opposite end of the office, the view from the lawyer's end of the office where Bartleby is stationed, are windows looking out on the blackened wall of a tall adjacent building. The space between the two buildings looks like a cistern or, one might conclude, a grave. Clerks, like those in the narrator's office, face metaphoric blank walls all their lives: the wall of business to which they are sacrificed and the blank walls of their careers and lives that lock them into poverty-wage positions.

In the narrator's chambers are two work rooms, one occupied by Turkey and Nippers and one occupied by the lawyer–narrator and his alter ego, Bartleby. The scriveners' quarters include tables for each to write on. These could have been high slanted desks. The tools of each scrivener include ink, inkstands, blotters, something like a quill to act as a pen, knives for sharpening pens, stores of blank white and blue paper, and piles of completed documents. In this room, Ginger-Nut, the office boy, has a small desk that he rarely uses. This room is also an entrance where a variety of colleagues, clients, witnesses, and messengers enter the chambers and congregate to do business, making the chambers "hum" with "industry and life." Toward the end of each day, as the sun sets, they work by candlelight.

The second room is the lawyer's private office, separated from the main copyists' room by glass doors. Bartleby is placed behind a folding screen in the lawyer's office. There is a "rickety old sofa" in this room which the narrator discovers has been serving as Bartleby's bed. The meanness of Bartleby's existence is also revealed in the contents of his desk: a blanket, a box for shining shoes, and ginger nuts on which he appears to live. On a chair, the narrator finds a wash basin, soap, and towel.

A SCRIVENER'S WORK

An army of clerks worked for lawyers, stock brokers, and other businesspeople in big financial centers like London and New York. Although the work was considered a step up from physical labor, the work of a copyist was grueling and demanding. In the narrator's law office, the primary activity was the drawing up of original legal and business documents and the many copies required by the business. The documents could run to 500 pages. At this time in the nineteenth century, there was no computer, no photocopier, no typewriter, and no reliable carbon paper. Nor were there pens that held ink. The quill used for writing had to be dipped constantly in the ink well. Thus, each document, "closely written in a crimpy hand," had to be copied out laboriously and meticulously by hand and each copy—usually as many as four—had also to be written out by hand. Within a week of his joining the office, Bartleby completed at least four 500-word documents.

The second part of the job was equally arduous. Especially with legal documents, like the ones created in the narrator's office, absolute accuracy was imperative. A misplaced comma, an extra zero, an omitted word could make the difference in thousands of dollars. So one of the most despised duties was verifying "the accuracy of ... copy, word by word." The narrator describes this work as a "very dull, wearisome, and lethargic affair." To some people, he admits, it would be "intolerable" (12). Often, this would require checking quadruplicate copies. If only one scrivener was available, he had to proof the original he had written as well as the copies, one by one, by himself. On days when another scrivener and the lawyer were available, the copyist had help in the process—one reading from the original while the others checked the copies. Even Ginger Nut joined in this work.

The copyists worked from early morning until six o'clock at night for six days a week. They were not paid regular salaries. Nor were they paid by the hour. Instead they were paid $.04 per 100 words. So, for Bartleby's 500-word, quadruplicate document, he received $2.80. The copyists were not paid for proofreading. Nor were they paid for documents that had to be recopied because of blots or errors. So Turkey, who makes ink blots on documents after twelve o'clock noon, makes little if any money in the afternoon. "As Nippers once observed, Turkey's money went chiefly for red ink" (9). Ginger Nut was paid one dollar a week.

THE CLERKS' POVERTY

Clerks in offices were regarded as somehow superior to factory workers and to all those who worked with their hands. The higher position these workers occupied was denoted by their dress. The factory worker—called a blue-collar worker—dressed in casual, roomy work clothes like overalls, which were often soiled with dirt, soot, and lint or stained with oil and chemicals. But the Wall Street clerk was required to dress more formally in black suits, ties, polished shoes, and white shirts, hence the label, "white-collar worker." The narrator expects his clerks to have a "gentlemanly sort of deportment" (8).

But despite the office worker's higher status, he was still doomed to poverty with his $.04 per hundred words. Turkey's poverty is especially pathetic in that he is reaching old age. The narrator is ashamed of Turkey's grease-stained clothes, finally coming to the conclusion that Turkey could simple not afford decent clothes on "so small an income" (9). The implication is that Turkey rents a cheap room to live in and has his meals in cheap eating houses.

The younger Nippers also makes poverty-level wages that he cannot possibly live on. So he does freelance legal work. Still he accrues debts, and bill collectors call on him at the office.

The narrator is also forced to acknowledge Bartleby's poverty, which (along with his phobia) has led him to sleep in the office and live entirely on little cakes called ginger nuts. Six or eight ginger nuts can be purchased for a penny. After the narrator first discovers that Bartleby sleeps in the office, he exclaims, "His poverty is great; but his solitude, how horrible!" Bartleby's poverty is perceived as a contrast to "the bright silks and sparkling faces" the narrator had seen on Wall Street and Broadway the same day. The lawyer, however, insists that, technically, Bartleby supports himself. Still, the narrator concedes that after Bartleby's release from the Tombs, where he has been taken on a charge of vagrancy, he will likely be admitted to the poorhouse.

WORKERS' HOPELESSNESS

The hopelessness of the scrivener's situation, the impossibility of advancement, is a critical work issue in many nineteenth-century positions, for both blue and white collar workers. White-collar positions other than clerical work were limited. The narrator recites the few possibilities that he thinks Bartleby might be suitable for: bartender, bill collector, or gentleman's traveling companion.

The hopelessness of a dead-end job in which no advancement is possible is most apparent in the case of Nippers. Some law clerks, like Ginger Nut, had families with enough money to place them with lawyers to study law until they could go out on their own. Others, like the narrator's three scriveners, are doomed to copy their whole life. Nippers is sufficiently responsible and knowledgeable to be left in charge of the narrator's business for a few days when the lawyer escapes in his rockaway. But Nippers, despite his capabilities and ambition, has no chance of advancement. He will quite likely always be a copyist making $.04 per hundred words, until he is an old man like Turkey. Nippers sees his real future everyday in Turkey. But, at 25 years old, Nippers grasps at opportunities, attempting as he does to act the lawyer on his own and play around in local politics. There is no doubt, however, that deep down, he realizes that his hopes for the future are unfounded.

THE EFFECT OF WORK ON HEALTH

All three of the narrator's copyists have been deeply damaged by the jobs they have been doomed to perform. Overwork and pollution from machinery caused bodily harm to factory workers. Clerical workers escaped these sorts of injuries and ailments, but were not exempt from psychological and physical damage as a direct result of poverty and hopelessness.

Turkey, an Englishman locked in the position of copyist, even in his old age, alleviates his misery with alcohol, chiefly imbibed at the noon dinner break. Afterward he is noisy, impatient, and unproductive. The purchase of alcohol out of his meager wages leaves him without the simple necessities of life, like warm, decent clothes.

Whereas Turkey's physical and psychological problem is alcoholism, Nippers, even in his young years, has developed what appears to be stomach ulcers, the symptoms of which show themselves in the morning before he has eaten, when his stomach is empty and churning with acid. Whereas the alcoholic Turkey goes into a passion over his blots in the afternoon, Nippers becomes furious over the height of his desk in the morning. The narrator correctly observes that Nippers did not know what he wanted, unless "it was to be rid of a scrivener's table altogether" (8).

Bartleby, supposedly having worked in an emotionally draining job as a clerk in the Washington, DC, dead letter office and as a clerk in other positions, has also been deeply psychologically wounded by what he has observed of the human condition and what he knows of this society's regard for him and demands of him. Even as soon as he joins the law chambers, the narrator observes his odd, unsociable, emotionless character. His eccentricities become increasingly apparent when he refuses to check copy or run errands. It is the youth Ginger Nut who first calls him "luny," The reader discovers the extent of Bartleby's problem (which the ironic narrator himself does not fully acknowledge) when he discovers that Bartleby never leaves the building. He suffers from a phobia that makes him too fearful to leave the office, and he must finally be escorted to jail by the police.

As business flourishes, these workers constantly resist being turned into automatons, writing down, over and over, words not their own, deprived by poverty of natural lives. The narrator's own words in the final paragraph of the story sums up the problem. He writes that dead letters sound like dead men. "On errands of life, these letters [read "men"] speed to death" (46). So the literal letters of the dead letter office, that have been sent on errands of hope—money, proposals of marriage, apologies, forgiveness—have been undeliverable and end in the dead letter office to be burned. The workers are like the dead letters. They have been born to create, to aspire, to love and be loved, but in this society they do not create—they copy other men's words. They cannot aspire, for their jobs are dead ends. They cannot have the love of wives and children because they are too poor.

WORKER REBELLION

In 1848, five years before Melville wrote "Bartleby, the Scrivener," Karl Marx and Friedrich Engels shocked the world in their *The Communist*

Manifesto by calling on workers to revolt. Revolts on the part of factory workers against a variety of problems like long hours and low wages had arisen in the United States in the 1840s. But no such organized revolts touched the white-collar workers, who saw themselves as having a higher status than people who worked with their hands.

But as "Bartleby, the Scrivener" illustrates, small personal insurgencies were not unknown among office workers. Turkey's revolts against his poverty and the deadliness of his job are the first instances introduced in the tale. Fortified by alcohol, he storms back into the office after lunch, blotting with ink the documents that are the bane of his life, turning over his sand box, splitting his pens and scattering them on the floor. Turkey's rebellion is also seen in what his employer calls "insolence," impertinence, and rashness. When the narrator asks him to work only half a day, he refuses. When the lawyer gives him an old, cast-off coat, he gloats. Nippers has his own revolts, chiefly regarding his desk. He grinds his teeth, hisses maledictions, and slams around his desk.

The revolts of Turkey and Nippers in the first of the narrative prepare for the later, more significant revolt of Bartleby. Their courses of action become identified as the rebellions that they are, when both men begin echoing Bartleby's words in passive protest: "I prefer not to." At times the narrator becomes worried that Bartleby's audacity will infect his other employees.

Bartleby, of course, is the real rebel, even in his passivity. He is the original sit-down striker, refusing to do the work for which he has been hired, beginning with what even his boss describes as the deadliest job of proofreading.

Every aspect of this unbridled capitalistic society denies its workers life and full humanity. Bartleby's firm answer is, in effect, if this is what the world has in store for me, I prefer not to.

BARTLEBY'S DESCENDANTS: DEHUMANIZATION AND RESISTANCE

The number of clerical workers has increased tenfold since the time of Bartleby. Clerical work has been revolutionized by the introduction of an overwhelmingly female clerical force, the invention of the typewriter, and the development of the computer. But issues raised by Melville in "Bartleby, the Scrivener" are as applicable to the twenty-first century as they were to the 1850s. The introduction of office machines and the speed-up have done even more to diminish the individualism and full humanity of workers who have come, increasingly, to be less important than the machine, becoming, in effect, extensions of the machine. First the typewriter and, later, the computer have come to stand between the worker and the finished product.

Individualism, privacy, and freedom are curtailed by the setup of many offices—huge rooms with scores of workers assigned to rows and rows of desks in the middle, while division managers around the edge of the room, at desks facing the workers, monitor them, often insisting on the same speed-ups that plagued factory workers.

Social interaction and human communication were severely hindered by the introduction of office cubicles in which employees work, not with each other, but solely with their computers. Bartleby's blank wall is replaced in the twenty-first century by the three blank walls of the present-day cubicle. The uniformity and conformity of the mass office situation and the cubicle seem to complete the workers' transformation into automatons.

The divisions of labor in all aspects of clerical and factory work have further served to separate the worker from the product he or she labors on. In the contemporary office, for example, functions are divided into discrete specialties, taking away any interest and pride in a finished project. Some workers are the bookkeepers, some the receptionists, some the programmers, some the word processors. Nothing so parallels this principle, the mechanical and impersonal "spiritual" death of a lifetime of copying and correcting documents, as the factory's assembly line, refined by Henry Ford. The following is from David Gartman's essay, "Origins of the Assembly Line and Capitalist Control of Work at Ford":

> Since its origin, the assembly line has been killing auto workers in a number of ways. Death might come in the literal form of an industrial accident on the relentless, driving line, as it did recently at a GM assembly plant in California. Or it might be the "spiritual" death brought on by a lifetime of boring, monotonous, and meaningless work. The assembly line has also meant the death of an important aspect of working-class power, for it has been a crucial factor in the demise of a tradition of skilled, intelligent labor. (193)

As in Bartleby's day, the clerical worker can rarely aspire to better jobs within the organization, for positions in management generally require advanced degrees: MAs, MBAs, CPAs, or law degrees. Thus, any move the office worker makes is usually lateral. One thing that contributed to this in the early twentieth century was that most clerical positions were, by that time, occupied by women, and even a woman with an education was not deemed suitable for any management position.

The resistance of Bartleby in Melville's tale is a precursor of the sit-down strike in American factories, a more passive form of labor action than was especially prominent in the 1930s, but has continued to be used, in both political and labor disputes, into the twenty-first century. A sit-down occurs when farm or factory workers refuse to work or to vacate the workplace, thus bringing the entire operation to a halt. So effective were the sit-down strikes in the 1930s—like the one in Flint, Michigan's General Motors plant—that the owners were successful in having government outlaw them.

In the twentieth and twenty-first centuries, one finds considerable resistance, not just on the effort of organized labor, but, as in Bartleby's day, on the part of individual workers, acting independently—sometimes carefully planned and sometimes done almost unconsciously. This has given rise to the term *skippy*, meaning an action on the part of an individual worker that jeopardizes the quality of the work he or she is intended to produce. In industry, a skippy occurs when a worker on an assembly line fails to insert a vital screw into a piece of machinery like an auto part. It is also called *sabotage*, a means by which one or several workers destroy the product or bring the machinery to a halt. It derives from the French word for wooden shoe, *sabot*, which angry workers once threw into machinery to bring it to a halt. In an act of sabotage, a worker will place something in the machinery that will cause it to break down. While the broken machinery is getting repaired, the workers are able to have a rest. Perhaps in a textile mill, a worker will put vinegar into a loom for weaving silk, ruining the entire batch. Or a dock worker might "accidentally" drop a crate of fragile goods.

In Bartleby's day, the response on behalf of disgruntled office workers was somewhat different. The defiance of Turkey and Nippers at being dehumanized is almost unconscious, and both men see themselves as gentlemanly professionals who are part of the system. These clerks would likely have viewed the protests of the textile girl workers in Lowell, Massachusetts, in the 1840s, as abhorrent. In the twentieth and twenty-first centuries, many office workers have very rarely organized to redress their grievances, seeing themselves as more aligned with management than labor. But often individual office workers turn to sabotage, something of an underground secret of the business world. Sometimes, it is reported, the sabotage of office workers is something they might not be fully, intellectually aware of doing. But at other times office sabotage is carefully planned in response to a slight on the part of a manager, to having been passed over for a raise, or to having been loaded up with extra work.

Sabotage occurs in insurance offices, banks, law offices, and brokerage houses. Turkey blots his documents; Nippers slams around his desk and hisses; Bartleby refuses to work and refuses to move. The present-day disgruntled office resister might hack into a payroll, causing it to disappear and infect the businesses entire payroll. A paralegal might collect money to pay the clients' doctors but pocket most of the rest of the money that should have gone to the law firm. An insurance file clerk might let the paperwork for a policy go through even though the client has not kept up the premiums. A clerk working for a cosmetics company might leave the office early but put in for a full day's work. A court clerk might destroy notices of court appearances. The possibilities are endless.

"Bartleby, the Scrivener," in its depiction of workers whose independence, creativity, individualism, and aspirations are wiped out by the scramble for profit, is as timely in the twenty-first century as it was in 1853.

QUESTIONS AND PROJECTS

1. Scholars have often radically disagreed about the character of the narrator, some viewing him as the hero of the piece who has an enlightenment at the end, others regarding him as seriously flawed from beginning to end. Have a classroom debate on the character of the narrator. Consider how one's view of him affects one's interpretation of Bartleby and the situation of the clerks.

2. Melville seems to have been influenced by a short portrait of the clerk, Nemo, in Charles Dickens's *Bleak House*. Read "The Law Writer," in which Nemo is mentioned, and make a written report on Nemo's situation and its pertinence to "Bartleby, the Scrivener." Could Nemo be a model for Turkey?

3. Melville, in his theme of the worker on Wall Street, makes a point of mentioning John Jacob Astor. Do some research of your own on Astor and write a paper explaining why you think Melville included him in "Bartleby, the Scrivener."

4. The lawyer who tells the story has generally been regarded as an ironic narrator—one who reveals to the hearer more than he

actually realizes. Write a paper on what the narrator reveals that
he probably does not grasp himself.

5. Do some research on the definition and history of capitalism and
   write a paper on your findings.
6. Why do you think Melville was so meticulous in his description
   of the workplace and the scriveners' duties?
7. Do a survey of a few downtown blocks devoted to business in
   your area. Find out how many clerks, receptionists, accountants,
   word-processors, and so on work in the two-block area and what
   their jobs are, their approximate ages, and their past work experiences. Make your report in the form of a chart.
8. Each student should conduct an in-depth, anonymous interview
   with an office worker, keeping Bartleby in mind. Have a classroom discussion beforehand to arrive at key questions regarding salary, lack of advancement, boredom, work-related health
   problems, and expressions of dissatisfaction. Upon editing your
   work, do everything possible to disguise the identity of your interviewee. Make a book of the collection of interviews for your local
   library.
9. In the 2004 political campaign, the subject of "two Americas"
   arose on several occasions. Would you say that "Bartleby, the
   Scrivener" presents two Americas? Why or why not?

FURTHER READING

Ayo, Nicholas. "Bartleby's Lawyer on Trial." *Arizona Quarterly* 28 (1972):
     27–38.
Barnett, Louise K. "Bartleby as Alienated Worker." *Studies in Short Fiction*
     11 (1974): 379–85.
Berthoff, Warner. ed. *Great Short Works of Herman Melville*. New York:
     Harper and Row, 1969.
Campbell, Marie A. "A Quiet Crusade: Melville's Tales of the Fifties,"
     American Transcendental Quarterly 7 (1970): 8–12.
Cochran, Thomas C. and William Miller. *The Age of Enterprise*. New York:
     Macmillan and Co., 1951.
Cohen, Hennig. "Bartleby's Dead Letter Office." *Melville Society Abstracts*
     10 (1972): 5–6.
D'Avanzo, Mario L. "Melville's 'Bartleby' and John Jacob Astor." *New England
     Quarterly* 41 (1968): 259–64.

Dickens, Charles. *A Christmas Carol*. London: Chapman and Hall, 1843.

Dillingham, William B. *Melville's Short Fiction*. Athens, GA: University of Georgia Press, 1977.

Fisher, Marvin. *Going Under: Melville's Short Fiction and the American 1850s*. Baton Rouge, LA: Louisiana State University Press, 1977.

Fogle, Richard Harter. *Melville's Shorter Tales*. Norman, OK: University of Oklahoma Press, 1960.

Gartman, David. "Origins of the Assembly Line and Capitalist Control of Work at Ford." *Case Studies of the Labor Process*. Ed. Andrew Zimbalist. New York: Monthly Review Press, 1979.

Hardwick, Elizabeth. "Bartleby and Manhattan." *New York Review of Books*. July 16, 1981: 27–31.

Inge, M. Thomas, ed. *Bartleby the Inscrutable: A Collection of Commentary on Herman Melville's Tale "Bartleby, the Scrivener."* Hamden, CT: Archon Books, 1979.

McTague, Michel J. *The Businessman in Literature*. New York: Philosophical Library, 1981.

Melville, Hermann. *Bartleby, the Scrivener: A Story of Wall Street*. New York: Simon and Schuster, 1997.

Newman, Lea Bertani Vozar. *A Reader's Guide to the Short Stories of Herman Melville*. Boston: G.K. Hall, 1986.

Orchard, B.G. *The Clerks of Liverpool*. Liverpool, UK: J. Collinson, 1871.

Pessen, Edward. *Riches, Class, and Power before the Civil War*. Lexington, MA: D.C. Heath and Company, 1973.

Randall, John H., III. "Bartleby vs Wall Street: New York in the 1850s." *Bulletin of the New York Public Library* 78 (1975): 138–44.

Rogin, Michael Paul. *Subversive Genealogy*. New York: Knopf, 1983.

Smith, Matthew. *Sunshine and Shadow*. Hartford, CT: J.B. Burr, 1869.

Sprouse, Martin, ed. *Sabotage in the American Workplace*. San Francisco: Pressure Drop Press, 1992.

Thomas, Brook. "The Legal Fictions of Herman Melville and Lemuel Shaw." *Critical Inquiry* 11 (1984): 24–51.

Vincent, Howard P., ed. *A Symposium: Bartleby the Scrivener*. Kent, Ohio: Kent State University Press, 1966.

Weeks, Charles A. "Bartleby's Descendents: The Theme of the White-Collar Worker in Modern Literature," *Dissertation Abstracts* 40 (1979): 4584A.

Zinn, Howard. *The People's History of the United States*. New York: HarperPerennial, 1995.

6

Upton Sinclair's *The Jungle*

In 1904, after a failed strike in the Chicago meatpacking industry, 26-year-old Upton Sinclair, a young man from a wealthy family and a recent convert to socialism, traveled to the community in Chicago called Packingtown. He lived there for seven weeks among the immigrant workers in the largest meatpacking industry in the United States. *The Jungle*, the novel he wrote growing out of his experiences, graphically describes work there in Chicago in 1904 and raises horrific but continuing workplace issues. Considered by many to be the most powerful social argument in an age of muckraking literature, *The Jungle* had been written as a brief for the working man. It did stun the public, including the president of the United States, Theodore Roosevelt. But the reforms it inspired had little or nothing to do with the condition of the workers. Instead, it instigated reforms in the way meat was slaughtered, packed, and inspected. The direct result was the passage of the Pure Food and Drug Act and the Meat Inspection Act, both signed into law on June 30, 1906, only months after the novel's publication in the same year. Sinclair later said that he had written the novel to touch the public's heart and instead had hit it in the stomach.

The issues developed in *The Jungle* are so extensive that its main character, Jurgis, is sometimes presented as symbolic of all those who labor with their hands in a system of rampant capitalism. The primary problems of the immigrant workers in the novel include the following:

- long hours and poverty-level wages
- the resultant squalid living conditions

- hazards in the workplace: disease and accidents
- the insecure and seasonal nature of the work
- child labor
- immigrant labor
- speed-ups
- lack of medical or unemployment compensation, retirement funds, and other safety nets
- sexual harassment
- homelessness
- political corruption
- unions, strikes, and scabs
- blacklisting

AN IMMIGRANT'S STORY

At the turn of the twentieth century, a group of Lithuanians, two families soon to be related by marriage, had seen their world fall apart in Eastern Europe, where jobs were scarce and men lived under the threat of abduction by the military. They found hope in promises of work issued by packing houses in Chicago in recruitment pamphlets and by rumors and stories of riches and freedom passed to them by relatives and friends who lived in the United States. The constant refrain repeated then (and now) is that one can always find work in Chicago.

The main members of the family consist of Jurgis Rudkus (the protagonist of *The Jungle*), his father Antanas, his fiancée Ona, Ona's brother Jonas, her Aunt Marija, her stepmother Teta Elzbieta, and Elzbieta's children.

The money they accumulate for their passage dwindles rapidly as they are cheated by officials on board ship and by immigration authorities in New York City. Their chosen destination is the stockyards in Chicago called Packingtown, where they have been told that jobs are plentiful and wages high. What the family finds out immediately is that the whole country is in the throes of a depression that has thrown thousands out of work and that the wages they will be paid will not allow them to meet the expenses, which are much higher than they anticipated. They find a large community made up entirely of poor immigrants, chiefly Lithuanians and Poles, who, in their own extreme poverty, are as supportive as they can be. With the help of one old friend, who has long been established in Packingtown, they are given a tour of their prospective workplace and the name of a boardinghouse.

The place where Jurgis and Jonas expect to find jobs is a hellish place, whose center is appropriately named "the killing floors." The farther they reach into the heart of the factories, the smokier, dingier, and darker it becomes. There is no living plant, no grass, not even weeds, growing in the entire area. The odor from the killing fields is penetrating and nauseating. The sounds of thousands of cattle and pigs roaring and squealing, coupled with the thuds of cattle being hit by clubs, is deafening and unsettling. A two-block festering hole of garbage lies adjacent to the factories. Beside the walkways, fetid water pours down in deep rivulets which have to be crossed on planks. Near the center of Packingtown is a thirty-six square mile "yard" crammed with cattle as far as the eye can see.

The boardinghouse to which Jurgis and his family are sent on the day of their arrival is a filthy, dilapidated house where up to fourteen people live in a single room. Jurgis finds long lines of job-seekers at every section of every factory, many of whom have come back for months to stand in line for work.

Because Jurgis is so obviously strong, vigorous, and energetic, he secures a job on their second day in Chicago. He is to work sweeping entrails into traps in the floor and cleaning out the traps. Aunt Marija gets a job painting cans, and Jonas gets a job pushing heavy trucks inside a meatpacking plant. Their plan is to allow the young, prospective bride Ona and her stepmother to stay at home and to put Elzbieta's children in school.

But the family is taken in by crooked housing agents who prey on immigrants. Within the first month they find themselves overcome with monthly mortgage payments, interest payments, utility bills, payments for furnishings for the house, and necessary repairs to the rickety, old house they were told was new. Moreover, they find the house to be unheated and contaminated.

With these impossible financial burdens hanging over them, they agree that Ona and Elzbieta's fourteen-year-old son, Stanislovas, must seek employment as well. Ona bribes a foreman for a job in a basement sewing covers for hams.

After six months in Chicago's Packingtown, Jurgis and Ona are married with elaborate festivities that leave them $100 more in debt. Jurgis's aged father comes to the inevitable conclusion that he too must try to find work, but the hazardous environment at work and at home soon kill him.

It is Marija who first experiences the shock of learning that all work here is seasonal and insecure. They cannot depend on wages throughout the year. Jurgis also finds his work to be erratic. Some days he works for only two hours for a total of 35 cents. As housing expenses mount and income decreases, they freeze in their unheated house and are always on the edge of starvation. Ona, whose boss runs a brothel and whose foreman is a pimp, develops severe depression and anxiety after the birth of their son. As their second winter in the city approaches, Jonas deserts them without a word.

All workers at this time are subject to speed-ups, fewer hours, and lower wages. To make things worse, Jurgis slips on the bloody floor of his factory and so severely injures his ankle that he can't work at all for almost three months. Little Stanislovas, who has been deeply traumatized by witnessing an injury to a friend, comes home from work in the cold with his fingers frozen. He is permanently maimed and becomes so terrified that he must be forced to go to work in the cold alone. The 10- and 11-year-old boys are sent to downtown Chicago to sell newspapers and Elzbieta's sickly youngest child dies after eating Packingtown's contaminated sausage for breakfast. Jurgis, who finds and loses another job, finally secures work of the lowest kind in the fertilizer room. And Elzbieta must get a job; she becomes the slave of the sausage machine.

Jurgis, who had remained temperate in his use of alcohol, now begins drinking heavily. The family is also horrified by the news that Ona is again pregnant. Not long after, the family becomes aware that Ona has been forced into prostitution by her bosses. In a rage, Jurgis confronts Conner, her guilty foreman, and beats him senseless before he is pulled away from his victim and taken to jail. He spends Christmas Eve in jail and is later sentenced to 30 days. Young Stanislovas visits him in jail to report that the family is starving, Ona is very sick, an injured Marija has lost her job, Stanislovas cannot go to work in the snow, and rent and interest have come due.

When Jurgis finally gets out and reaches home, the house has new owners and his family has returned to the wretched boardinghouse where they first lived upon coming to Chicago. Upon reaching the boardinghouse, Jurgis finds Ona, barely 18 years old, and the baby dying in premature childbirth.

After the death of Ona and their second child, Jurgis, now blacklisted in Packingtown because of his assault on the politically connected Connor, goes uptown to look for enough work to care for his remaining son. After weeks of homelessness, the union finds him a job with Harvest Trust, making harvesting machines. But in the speed-ups, the men work too well, furnishing the world with all the harvesting machines it needs, and his department is abruptly closed. After another period of homeless-ness, he gets a job in a steel mill, far from the family, and suffers another accident. When he returns to his family, he finds that his little son, Antanas has gotten out of the boardinghouse and drowned in a massive hole of water by the street.

Jurgis leaves immediately, hitching a railroad car out into the country where, throughout the rest of the spring and summer, he works as a hobo on farms.

As fall approaches, he returns to downtown Chicago, holds a job briefly, and is sent to the hospital after being injured on the job. He is unable to return to work and receives no compensation. Eventually he is thrown out of his boardinghouse. Living on the street again without an overcoat in the bitter Chicago winter, Jurgis finds himself in jail again, where he encounters for the second time a dandified crook named Jack Duane. When Jurgis gets out of jail and hooks up with Duane, he is introduced to the high-class criminal world in Chicago. He helps commit armed robberies, beats up victims, sets up voting fraud, and takes part in a scheme to steal the local election for a Republican candidate.

When a strike is called by the meatpackers in Packingtown, he works actively as a scab and then as a boss, assisting the strike-breaking police. His downfall comes when he again encounters Connor, the man who had abused his wife, Ona. Jurgis once more beats him viciously and is arrested. But one of Jurgis's new friends gets him released from jail and tells him to run—to get away from the Irish bosses in Packingtown.

On the other side of Chicago, he is on the street again, trying to sleep on the stairs in the police station at night, eating, when he can, in soup kitchens, attending open meetings to warm up in the evenings. At this time, he runs into an old woman whom he once knew, who gives him Marija's address and tells him that Marija can help him. He finds her in a fancy house of prostitution that the police are in the process of raid-ing. She tells him she came here a year ago after she lost her job and the children were starving. Now Marija, a morphine addict and a prostitute, supports the remaining family. Jurgis returns to the streets, horrified by her story and too ashamed to go to his other relatives for help.

To keep warm for a while, Jurgis goes to the lecture hall again. This time the woman sitting next to him wakes him up and urges him to listen to what turns out to be a lecture on socialism. As he listens, he feels reborn and, along with many others, seeks out the speaker. Jurgis is able to get the speaker's attention and tells him briefly about his troubles. The man turns Jurgis over to another Lithuanian named Ostrinski who takes

Jurgis home, talks to him well into the night about socialism and the evils of capitalism, and lets Jurgis sleep on his kitchen floor.

Jurgis, who is reunited with Elzbieta, finds a job as a porter in a hotel, only to discover happily that his boss and workmates are also socialists. Back on his feet, Jurgis actively works, even publicly speaks for the cause of socialism. It becomes his whole life, and he now exists in the world of ideas. His attempt to rescue Marija fails and, although he is unhappy at home because of Elzbieta's illness and the wildness of the boys, he stays with them and stands by them.

Chapters 28–31 are careful outlines of what socialism means and the various arguments for and against it. The novel ends on Election Day, when Jurgis and his comrades ecstatically meet in the lecture hall to celebrate the immense growth of the Socialist Party in the United States.

THE HISTORICAL CONTEXT OF THE JUNGLE

The Jungle is set in the greatest era of unbridled capitalism and labor struggle in the United States. Fifty years before the action of the novel, the Civil War, itself, was an impetus to business. A sudden and overwhelming need arose for more extensive railroads, uniforms, shoes, cannons, guns, and ammunition, among other things, to supply to the soldiers. New inventions revolutionized and speeded up the production of goods: the Bessemer steelmaking process and the steam-run machines that facilitated digging for coal, for example. The war provided a handful of men an opportunity to gain economic ascendancy, often making their first fortunes by defrauding the American people with the help of the government. One example was the young banker, J. P. Morgan, who managed to escape service in the Civil War by paying another person $300 to fight in his place. During the war Morgan bought 5,000 rifles for $3.50 apiece and then sold them to the U.S. Army for $20 a piece. By 1890, Morgan was not only a banking tsar; he had total control of four of the six railway systems in the United States. Philip Armour, a prominent member of the Beef Trust, fictionalized by Upton Sinclair in *The Jungle*, began making his fortune during the war by buying beef for $18 a barrel and selling it to the army for $40. This one transaction netted him $2,000,000. Other prominent magnates included Andrew Carnegie, who controlled U.S. Steel, and John D. Rockefeller, who controlled the oil industry.

By exploiting impoverished workers in the United States, Asia, and Europe, power in the hands of men whom history has labeled robber barons was solidified and monopolized after the war. Their fortunes could not have been so great without the help of state and local legislatures, the U.S. Congress, and the courts. Thomas Edison, for example, bribed New Jersey lawmakers for legislation favorable to him and his inventions. And the railroads paid millions of dollars in bribes to appropriate land belonging to others.

Monopolies flourished, putting production in the hands of fewer and fewer corporations. Meanwhile the U.S. Supreme Court successfully undermined all legislation to keep monopolies in check, at the same time that they ignored the rights of workers to unionize and strike. Historian Howard Zinn quotes a New York banker who in 1895 praised the court as the "guardian of the dollar, defender of private property" (254).

To force competition for work and ensure low wages, immigrants were lured to the United States, pouring into the country in the final decades of the nineteenth and early twentieth centuries. The large meatpacking monopolies, jointly called the Beef Trust, had routinely sent lures in the form of pamphlets to Poland and Lithuanian asking for workers, whom they suspected would be more acquiescent and work for lower wages than U.S. citizens. The Durham plant in the novel, for instance, advertised for 200 workers in the family's first year in Chicago. Of the 800 who came to apply for jobs, Durham hired only 20people. Great numbers of Irish and Germans had entered the country earlier in the century. By 1880, there were 75,000 Chinese laborers working in California alone. In the next three decades immigrants from Eastern Europe were arriving in the largest numbers. By 1890, there were 4million immigrant workers in the United States, often lured by false promises of work, whose presence brought down the wages of existing laborers and allowed the barons to increase hours and refuse to ameliorate working conditions. In the last decades of the nineteenth century, 1,118,000 children under the age of 16 years were working in United States factories.

The exploitation of working men, women, and children finally led to strikes and demonstrations throughout the country, some preceding the organization of labor into unions. Following is a partial list of the more prominent strikes between 1884 and 1904.

1884:	Textile workers and hat makers in New York City
1885:	Cloak and shirt makers in New York City
1885:	2,500 women carpet weavers in Yonkers
1886:	Railroad workers on the Texas and Pacific Railroad
1886:	General strike of 350,000 workers nationwide

1886:	10,000 sugar workers in Louisiana
1891:	Miners working for Texas Coal Mine Co.
1891:	20,000 in a general strike in New Orleans
1892:	Copper miners in Coeur d'Alene, Colorado.
1892:	3,000 steel workers at Homestead, Pennsylvania
1894:	Railroad workers at the Pullman Company, near Chicago
1899:	Miners in Salt Lake City and Coeur d'Alene
1901:	Miners at Telluride, Colorado
1903:	Miners at Cripple Creek, Colorado
1904:	Meat packers in Chicago

By 1904, union membership had soared to 2,072,200.

Two momentous events in the last decades of the nineteenth century formed the background of conflict between labor and capital in Chicago that surfaces in *The Jungle*. The first was the Haymarket affair of May 1886. Industrial workers in Chicago held small, angry demonstrations in the spring of 1886, seeking a raise in wages and an eight-hour day. Albert R. Parsons and August Spies, Chicago labor leaders, encouraged a strike on May 1. It was a day of peaceful parades and speeches. But in the next week, police shot in the back locked-out strikers at McCormick Harvester Works and killed six of them. (Jurgis works at a fictionalized version of this company for a brief time.)

On May 4, a meeting was called for Haymarket Square in Chicago for the purpose of having Parsons and Spies speak to a group of seamstresses who wanted to organize. It also was a calm and peaceable gathering. But then 180 Chicago police began barging into the crowd, swinging clubs and ordering the crowd to disperse. Suddenly a bomb was thrown into the crowd, and eight policemen were killed.

No one could really determine the source of the bomb. The owners, police, and the general public insisted that one of the workers had thrown it. The workers were just as certain that one of the irresponsible vigilantes hired by the owners had thrown the bomb as a provocation.

The press, owners, and police turned their ire toward all foreigners and immigrants, many of whom were common laborers and were suspected of having introduced radical social theories into the United States. Seven labor leaders were arrested, tried, found guilty of murder, and sentenced to death. Four men were hanged in November of 1887. John Peter Altgeld, a German immigrant, after becoming governor of Illinois, researched the case meticulously and chose to pardon the three remaining men on death row, an act of political suicide.

The second event that set the tone of worker defiance in Chicago was the Pullman Strike of 1894. Pullman, Illinois, was a company town in the suburbs of Chicago where 5,000 workers were employed in the making of sleeping cars for trains. Not only did the Pullman Company pay its workers starvation wages, it had devised a plan whereby it would retrieve all the wages it paid out. The first step in the plan was to require all workers to live in company housing in the company town, buy goods from the company stores, and buy utilities from the Pullman company. Then Pullman charged its workers much higher prices than were standard elsewhere. Rents in Pullman were 20 to 25 percent higher than comparable units elsewhere in the area, for example, and Pullman charged its employees at the rate of $2.25 per thousand cubic feet for gas, which the company had bought at the rate of 33 cents per thousand cubic feet.

Driven to desperation, many of them starving, the workers in 1894 secretly joined the American Railway Union (ARU) that had been founded in the previous year. After several negotiations with Pullman failed, the workers struck in May of that year, and the larger ARU members agreed to support them. By June 29, there were 125,000 railroad workers out on strike, and 15 railroads and the U.S. mails were being held up.

On June 30 at night, 1,000 U.S. marshals, who had been sent to Chicago, opened fire into crowds of peaceful demonstrators and set fire to property. By early July, 14,000 armed police, company marshals, and soldiers were in the Chicago area to enforce an injunction, declaring that the strike was illegal. In the ensuing violence that broke the strike, 30 men and women were killed, and 100, most of them peaceful bystanders, were injured. One hundred twenty thousand workers were blacklisted.

Against this backdrop, the owners of the meatpacking industry grew to be the largest employer of workers in the country, and the meat packers themselves struggled for a decent survival. With the growth of industrialization and mechanization in the nineteenth century, the nature of meat processing changed. No longer was it carried out on small farms or in small businesses; instead, it came to be concentrated in Midwestern cities. In the 1850s meatpacking shifted to Chicago, an ideal place for manufacturing, with its location on Lake Michigan and its accessibility by rail. With the development of refrigerated railroad cars in the 1870s, Chicago corporations secured the lion's share of the meatpacking market. By the 1880s, with the wholesale manufacture of more reliable refrigerator cars by Swift and other meat companies, more efficient butchering and meatpacking could be done close to the source of beef and hog raising, and Chicago meatpacking replaced that which had been done in the East. Between 1870 and 1890, growth in the meatpacking industry was 900 percent, and it came to be Chicago's biggest employer.

The meatpacking companies in the late nineteenth century joined to form one of the largest monopolies in the United States. In 1886, it was investigated by the federal government but no changes were made. In 1887, the passage of the Interstate Commerce Act cemented their combined power in that it favored large shippers, like the Beef Trust, to the detriment of the railroads. In 1890, the Sherman Anti-Trust Act was passed to break up and curb monopolies, but it had no effect on the meatpacking industry.

By the turn of the twentieth century, the owners of meatpacking businesses in Chicago were five in number: Swift, Armour, Morris, Cudahy, and Wilson. They came to be known as the Beef Trust. In 1902, Swift, Armour, and Morris established a unified corporation called the National Packing Company, with the aim of absorbing all the smaller meatpacking businesses.

The tremendous fortunes and power of these companies was built on the backs of workers whom they paid substandard wages and whom the companies used in the most brutal fashion to squeeze out every penny they could for themselves. With the advent of machines, the companies began using more and more unskilled labor and importing more eastern European workers. In the 1880s, some 27,300 workers were earning an average of $385 a year. Children under 16 years were put to work at $.04 an hour. In 1893 the country suffered a devastating depression and economic panic that lasted until 1897. The Swift Company cut wages 10 percent to keep its profits high. Wages at the turn of the century were from $.15 to $.185 an hour.

In light of worker abuse, objections, demonstrations, and strikes broke out among the workers. One of the first strikes occurred in 1885 when meat packers demanded an end to execrable working conditions. But their leader, Terence V. Powderly, a Knights of Labor official, made a secret accommodation with the owners that forced an end to the strike and a loss for the workers. In 1894, in response to the 10 percent cut in wages by Swift and others, the Chicago Stockyard Butchers Union, along with the American Railway Union, called for a general strike. But workers were easily replaced by scabs in a time of immense unemployment. In Chicago alone, 200,000 laborers were out of work. After the state militia was called in to quell worker violence against scabs, the strike failed. In 1896, the Amalgamated Meat Cutters and Butcher Workmen formed a national union, but it was successfully suppressed in Chicago. Workers in Packingtown were largely divided into numerous small unions from 1900 to 1903. Each of them conducted strikes of small groups of workers. From 1900 to 1902, there were 5 such strikes, and from 1903 to 1904, there were 36.

Then in January 1904, the country again fell into a catastrophic depression, leaving millions out of work. The larger, more inclusive Amalgamated Union was reorganized by Michael Donnelly, who called the strike, asking for a standard $.20 per hour for all workers. This is the strike fictionalized in *The Jungle*. The owners saw the strike not only as a demand for higher wages than they wanted to pay, but also as a strike that would determine who ran the various shops in the plants—the owners or the union. On July 12, the owners rejected the demand for $.20 per hour and 28,000 workers walked out. Of course, with such high unemployment, scabs were easily hired to take their places. On July 20, the owners again refused to raise wages or improve conditions but promised that there would be no discrimination against strikers in hiring. But on July 22, the deal fell apart when it was discovered that bosses *were* refusing to hire strikers. So the strike was on again.

Strikers attacked scabs, and police attacked strikers. The union provided food to strikers' families. On August 7, the union organized a parade of 20,000 men, women, and children. On that day, the speakers drew attention, not only to low wages, but to Packingtown's diseases, infant mortality, overcrowding, poverty, and polluted water.

On September 5, with strikers' families starving, the packers announced that, if the strike were called off, strikers would be reemployed. Owners refused any raise in salary. Finally, as strikers became more and more desperate, their families starving, they decided to go back to work. Union leaders were driven out and blacklisted and the union was broken.

For a time Jurgis and Marija are ardent members of the union. But after he has reached a low point, he serves as a scab during the 1904 strike. That which saves Jurgis is not the union, but socialism, which sometimes works in conjunction with the union. At the time of Jurgis's struggle in Chicago, the most prominent socialist leader in the United States was Eugene Debs, who became a convert to socialism in 1894 while serving time in jail. Jurgis learns that socialism is built on the idea of "common ownership and democratic management of the means of producing the necessities of life" (384); that the labor of millions of workingmen should not belong, as it did, to a few wealthy parasites; and that socialism would seize power from the capitalists and give it to the workers. In the election of 1904, socialists made considerable progress. Socialist James Ambrose was elected to the Illinois State Senate, and Packingtown emerged with the second highest vote for Eugene Debs on the Socialist Presidential ticket.

WORK IN PACKINGTOWN

Of all the exposés of capitalism's abuse of factory workers coming out of the first decade of the twentieth century, none has been so enduring or so graphic in its portrait of a variety of unskilled work within a massive industry as has Upton Sinclair's *The Jungle*. The two major meat processing corporations, called Durham and Brown's, are conglomerates incorporating many distinct functions: bringing in of cattle and putting them in the stockyard, slaughtering cattle and pigs, deboning them, butchering them, rending lard, loading railroad cars, labeling or painting cans of meat and lard, sewing cloth around hams, the making of fertilizer, pickling meat to be canned, and making glue, soap, candles, and other by-products.

THE SLAUGHTERHOUSE

Jurgis and his family's first view of work in Packingtown is the place where the animals—pigs, cattle, and sheep—are killed. Hogs go to the mechanized slaughter up a chute that narrows as it enters the killing room. Two men stand on either side of a massive wheel with rings around the edge. As the hogs reach the top of the building, the men quickly attach one end of a chain to the leg of a hog and the other end to one of the rings on the wheel. As each wheel descends, men slit the hogs' throats before a moving belt dumps them into boiling water. Machines remove the pigs from the boiling water, scrub off their bristles, and move them through two lines of men, each of whom has a specialized task, most of them having to use large knives to do such things as severing the head, slitting open the body, sawing the breast bone in two. The belt moves slowly but steadily and men work "as if a demon were after them" (41).

On another floor, in unbearable stench, men and women prepare the entrails for sausage casings, and in another area, workers sweep up scraps to be boiled for lard and soap. In several rooms, an army of men do the butchering of the chilled carcasses with massive cleavers.

In the cattle buildings, also working at the pace of machines, workers move animals from place to place using electric shocks. Others hit the cattle on the head with sledgehammers. The butchers work at top speed. "They worked [with knives and cleavers] with furious intensity, literally upon the run—a pace with which there is nothing to be compared except a football game" (44). Moving down 20 or so lines of carcasses, "[t]he floor was half an inch deep with [slippery] blood" (44). From there men with cleavers behead the beef, skin it, cut off the feet, and gut it before putting it in a chilling room, after which it is butchered and packed for shipment.

The rapid pace of men working with cleavers and knives on slippery floors is suggested by the number of animals processed: 10,000 cattle, 10,000 hogs, and 5,000 sheep each day, or 10 million animals a year.

THE FAMILY'S FIRST JOBS

Jurgis's first job is sweeping entrails in a hole in the floor, a hole so large it must immediately be covered to keep men from falling into it. Blood runs on the floor, and the stench is nauseating.

Marija's job involves continually lifting 14-pound cans all day long. The pace is killing, and she later finds that it is the most seasonal of work.

Jurgis's elderly father finds work in a pickling room. Here the workers stand in damp, cold cellars in salt water. The men put beef into vats of chemicals for canning, then remove it, and send it to the cooking room. Afterward they dump the vats of chemicals onto the floor. Antanas's job is to mop the chemicals into a sink in the floor that traps the refuse, dump out and shovel the refuse into containers with the rest of the meat.

Jonas works in an area where smoked hams are loaded onto huge iron trucks that are pushed through the room onto elevators. Each loaded truck weighs more than a quarter of a ton. Getting the truck moving on the uneven floor takes a massive effort.

When Marija loses her job as a can painter, she eventually finds one as a beef trimmer in another part of the canning factory. Her job is to trim hundreds of pounds of diseased beef from large cattle carcasses. In this job as in other meatpacking work, everything in the room is slippery with blood, including the knife she must use, working at top speed.

In the fertilizer room, where Jurgis finds his next job, the dust is so thick that the workers cannot see each other. The temperature in the room is over 100 degrees. Workers are given sponges to hold over their mouths.

The scariest work Jurgis has is not in the meatpacking industry, however, but in a steel mill, where huge white-hot beams of steel are crashed through the room, cauldrons of fiery steel bubbles all around the workers, and furnaces tend to explode, scattering their white-hot contents on workers.

Jurgis and his family come to the stockyards to get rich, but they are shocked to learn that wages are inadequate to meet basic expenses. Unions find that among unskilled workers, the highest wage is $14.00 a week and the lowest is $2.50 a week. Sinclair provides a catalog of wages throughout the novel. Jurgis, in his job sweeping up entrails, receives about $1.50 a day or about $9.00 a week. Can painters like Marija are paid $.14 per 110 cans and can make up to $12 a week. The highest paid of the family in the first year is Ona, who makes up to $30.00 a week. When Jurgis takes a job digging tunnels, he makes about $9.00 a week. In 1904, at the time of the strike, the average weekly salary on the killing floors was $6.50 a week.

The standard workweek is 72 hours, or 12 hours a day for six days. Workers in the stockyards during standard working hours are to show up at seven o'clock. If weather or other conditions make them as much as a minute late, they are docked for an entire hour. They work until seven at night. If, for some reason, work is halted before the last full hour ended, they are not paid for any portion of the hour. Hours are erratic. After the holiday rush, there might be no business, therefore no work at all. Sometimes in this slow period, they might work an hour or two. At other rush times, as when a big load of cattle comes in at the end of the day, they will be called upon to work as late as midnight, sometimes 15 or 16 hours a day with no additional pay for overtime.

Unskilled workers throughout the area have no job security, no unemployment safety net, no workers' compensation if they are injured on the job, no health insurance, and no retirement. If a worker is injured on the job, he usually finds when he returns to work after a period of recuperation, that his job has been given to someone else.

The chief curse of the workplaces in The Jungle is the speed-up. The more cattle that can be processed and the more goods produced in the least possible time meant lower labor costs and more money for the owners. Here Jurgis is first alarmed by the pace:

The pace they set here, it was one that called for every faculty of a man—from the instant the first steer fell till the sounding of the noon whistle, and again from half-past twelve til heaven only knew what hour in the late afternoon or evening, there was never one instant's rest for a man, for his hand or his eye or his brain.

Jurgis saw how they managed it; there were portions of the work which determined the pace of the rest, and for these they had picked men whom they paid high wages, and whom they changed frequently. You might easily pick out these pace-makers, for they worked under the eye of the bosses, and they worked like men possessed. This was called "speeding up the gang," and if any man could not keep up with the pace, there were hundreds outside begging to try. (64, 65)

The speed-ups, which strain every faculty of the worker, are apparent throughout the meatpacking industry, the company making farm machinery, and the steel mills. Not only does it exhaust the workers, it puts them in jeopardy for hurting themselves and others.

DANGERS ON THE JOB

One of the chief issues raised so graphically in *The Jungle* is the hazard of the workplace. The speed-ups and general disregard of all safety on the job, in pursuit of the almighty dollar, are the main causes of accidents. Workers are also made sick and killed by pollution, poisons, and caustic chemicals. In Jurgis's first job, where the floor is as slippery as bloody glass, men slip and fall, breaking arms and legs. The man who previously had lived in their house had been crushed against a pillar by a wounded steer. In the winter, steam in the room keeps the workers, frantic to avoid the steer, from seeing anything, including the knives wielded by other workers. Nor could the boss, who fires a gun to kill the rampaging steer, see what he was aiming at. The accidents that occur at these times are often fatal—from the steer, other people's knives, or the boss's bullets. Jurgis's first accident is slipping on the floor and severely hurting his ankle.

Standing all day, as Marija does, lifting 14-pound loads as a painter of cans also has its hazards as well. The lifting ruins the backs and internal organs of the women who work there, and the chemicals they breathe and get on their skin cause lung and skin damage.

Marija's second job as a beef boner is one of the most hazardous in the industry. Beef boners are paid by the piece, so they work as fast as they can for more money:

Your hands are slippery, and your knife is slippery, and you are toiling like mad, when somebody happens to speak to you, or you strike a bone. Then your hand slips up on the blade, and there is a fearful gash. (12)

The problem is not so much the cut itself but the inevitable blood infections that set in, sometimes laying up the worker for as long as seven months and sometimes requiring amputation of fingers or hands.

Poisonous fumes in the fertilizer rooms cause the workers to become dizzy and ill. Poisonous fumes and standing in brine that even eats through boots and feet leaves workers in the pickling room with fatal lung damage and sores that never heal.

In the area where Jonas works, the bosses kick and swear at the workers to move faster in pushing heavy iron trucks. The worker whose job Jonas took had been "jammed against the wall by one and crushed in a horrible" manner (71).

Men who work digging tunnels for phone lines die at the rate of one a day. Several are mangled each day by falling rock, collapsing foundations, and explosions. Severe injuries are also caused by falling from or being hit, as Jurgis is, by the railway cars carrying tons of rocks.

In the steel factory, Jurgis sees a man get his foot mashed off by a car crashing along with a load of heavy hot steel. Several weeks later, he sees a furnace, containing white hot steel, explode, "spraying two men with a shower of liquid fire" (237). They scream as their faces, clothes, and hands are on fire. Jurgis receives severe burns on his own hands after he tries to put out the fires burning the men.

The boy Stanislovas dies in the most horrible fashion in his workplace: One evening he falls asleep in a corner of an oil factory where he worked, is locked up when work stops at night, and is attacked and killed by rats, which eat him alive.

SEXUAL ABUSE AND PROSTITUTION

Another major issue in The Jungle is the sexual abuse of female workers and the economic desperation and brute force that entraps women into prostitution. Marija learns on her first day of work that the woman she is replacing had been seduced long ago and was the sole support of her son.

Ona learns shortly after she takes her job sewing up hams that her "forelady" is also a madam who runs a house of prostitution along with Connor, the boss of the loading gang at her workplace. Connor would "make free" (121) with the girls going in and out of the building, and the forelady would recruit girls working alongside Ona for prostitution. The narrator comments on the general situation with regard to women workers:

> But there was no place a girl could go in Packingtown, if she was particular about things of this sort; there was no place in it where a prostitute could not get along better than a decent girl. Here was a population, low-class and mostly foreign, hanging always on the verge of starvation, and dependent for its opportunities of life upon the whim of men, every bit as brutal and unscrupulous as the old-time slave-drivers; under such circumstances immorality was exactly as inevitable, and as prevalent, as it was under the system of chattel slavery. Things that were quite unspeakable went on there in the packing-houses all the time. (122)

Finally, Ona is told that she and every member of her family will be fired and blacklisted if she does not cooperate. At this point, after being harassed for months, Ona gives in.

When Jurgis joins forces with some Chicago criminals, he learns that thousands of girls are kidnapped, tricked, or driven by starvation into prostitution each year. From Europe and parts of the United States, they answer advertisements for servants and factory hands, only to find themselves abducted by employment agencies, drugged, raped, their clothes taken from them, and forced into prostitution.

After constant starvation and numerous injuries, Marija turns to prostitution as the only way to save the lives of the remaining children and Elzbieta. Jurgis learns about some cases from her. She tells him the story of six young French women. Only one of them escaped—by jumping from a two-story window to her death.

CHILD LABOR

In the early years of the twentieth century, a law was on the books prohibiting children under the age of 16 years from working in factories, but no one paid attention to it. Children barely in their teens could present dishonest documents to "prove" they were old enough to work. Because they could be paid half or one-third the wages of adults, factory bosses never questioned the veracity of these documents. An old woman tells Jurgis's family that the only change the law has made has been to cause people to lie about their children's ages.

Children like Stanislovas make about $.05 per hour in the factory. When it becomes apparent that 14-year-old Stanislovas would have to go to work, the local priest gives them a document claiming that he is the legal age of 16. In the factory, the young boy is kicked to keep him awake and to speed up his work. Each morning, Jurgis beats him to force him to go to work.

The youngest boys—10 and 11 years of age—must also finally be sent to work selling newspapers. They leave home for downtown Chicago at four in the morning and return late at night. All day long they are threatened with beatings by boys who are their competitors. They are also routinely robbed of their earnings. When the 13-year-old girl, Kotrina, must also leave the house where she has been babysitting, she is terrified by a man who tries to drag her into an alley. Afterward, she, too, must also be forced out of the house to work.

RELATED CURRENT ISSUES: SEXUAL HARASSMENT IN THE WORKPLACE

The Jungle calls attention to the blatant and brutal sexual abuse of workers at a time when the worker had little recourse against it except to starve. Today's women in free societies suffer nothing like the cruelty inflicted on what, in the early decades of the twentieth century, came to be called white, or factory, slaves. But sexual abuse and harassment have been a part of the workplace ever since. Factory girls and domestic workers, desperate for income, often found that they either had sex with their bosses or lost their livelihoods. Many more workers felt that their workplaces were made unbearable by the sexual advances and suggestive language of their bosses or coworkers. Those who resisted too often found themselves out of work, demoted, or blacklisted.

The situation of sexually harassed workers eventually changed with passage of the Civil Rights Act in 1964. In 1976, the United States Equal Employment Opportunity Commission found that, sexual harassment is a form of sex discrimination, in violation of Title Nine of the Civil Rights Act. Workers now had some legal recourse to sexual harassment on the job. In that year, 9 out of 10 female workers claimed in a survey by *Redbook* magazine that they had been the subjects of unwanted sexual advances on the job and, in 1980, 42 percent of female government workers and 15 percent of male government workers experienced some sort of sexual harassment. Complaints filed with the government regulating agency have increased substantially since the 1980s. The cost of harassment—which ranges from having to work in a hostile workplace to demands for prostitution—is psychologically injurious and damaging to the worker's reputation and career.

Ninety-five percent of sexual harassment is apparently never reported. But one high-profile case brought the problem to the public eye in 1991 when Oklahoma law professor Anita Hill, testified in the Supreme Court confirmation hearings of Clarence Thomas that he had consistently harassed her when she worked under his supervision, ironically, at the Equal Employment Opportunity Commission. Hill testified that Thomas had pressured her to date him, which she refused to do; had described sex acts to her; and had pressed pornographic films on her. Thomas was confirmed despite her testimony. Although the number of harassment cases doubled after the hearings (in 1996, e.g., 15,342 sexual harassment cases were filed), the Anita Hill case also illustrated that publicly raising harassment, especially against people in power, inevitably resulted in the vilification of the accuser.

Another accusation of sexual harassment in workplaces hit the head-lines in fall 2004 when a female producer working for Bill O'Reilly, a prominent Fox News commentator, accused him of harassing her with obscene phone calls. When she objected, she said, the phone calls became more frequent and more graphic in sexual content. Within the month, the case, strengthened by the plaintiff's tapes of O'Reilly's con-versations, was settled out of court.

A look at the cases filed in the first few days of January 2005 illustrates the persistence of sexual harassment cases and shows that, although the large majority of cases are filed by women against male employers and supervisors, some are filed against women, and some are filed by men. One involved the director of Florida's Elder Affairs. When a pattern of sexual harassment on his part was made known, he was fired on January 5, 2005. In the same week in Ohio, a judge attempted to fire several of his employees who charged him with sexual harassment. On January 7, California's state assembly paid an aide $49,000 after she charged that her boss, an assemblywoman, created a hostile work environment by press-ing the aide for details about her sex life and describing her own sex life to the aide. Also in the first week of January, in Shreveport, Louisiana, a male worker in a restaurant there charged its male owner with unwel-come sexual advances.

The sexual abuse to which workers were subjected in the early twentieth century is no longer accepted practice. But the pattern of harassment that occurs in work relationships of unequal power continues on, even as those who have been harassed at work have the legal right to complain. Still, complaining about harassment inevitably places personal reputation and one's profession at risk.

TWENTY-FIRST CENTURY ABUSES OF MEATPACKING EMPLOYEES

In January of 2005, Human Rights Watch, a watchdog group based in the United States, took the unusual step of singling out the meatpacking industry for criticism, indicating that working conditions were so abominable that the industry was violating the basic human rights of its workers as well as international treaties formed to protect workers. The substance of the investigation was reported by Steven Greenhouse of the *New York Times* on January 26, 2005 and was reinforced by a *Times* editorial on February 6, 2005.

The chief complaints against the owners were safety violations and the intimidation of unionized workers. Calling jobs in the meatpacking industry the most dangerous jobs in the United States, the report points out that there are 20 injuries for every 100 workers. The high speed on the line, the repetition of the same movement over 10,000 times a day, and the surfaces slippery with blood contribute to such injuries as the crushing of hands and even the cutting off of legs. Almost every worker interviewed for the report had suffered some serious physical injury.

Other hazards include asphyxiation from the fumes of rotting meat. Some studies indicate that one of the greatest dangers is infection from touching diseased carcasses.

The United States Department of Labor, in a 2004–05 handbook, agrees that meatpacking workers have the highest rate of injury of all other workers in the United States. Much of the reason for this is the dangerous equipment they must use: knives, cleavers, meat saws, and band saws. The Department of Labor also indicates that many in the industry have to work in cold rooms, damp with blood. Carpel tunnel syndrome and other ailments plague workers who have to perform repetitive tasks.

The Human Rights Watch report also draws attention to the industry's hiring of the most vulnerable people in the population—unskilled immigrants who will work for the lowest possible wages and have no knowledge of what their rights as workers are.

Attached to Steven Greenhouse's article in the *New York Times* are two photographs: one of a meatpacking plant in 1906 and one of a meatpacking plant in 2005. The notation for the photographs indicates that conditions since the publication of *The Jungle* have improved very little.

QUESTIONS AND PROJECTS

1. Write a history of Jurgis's and Ona's relationship. Indicate to what extent work and economics affect them.
2. Write a letter that Jurgis might send back to Lithuania advising a friend to either come to the United States or not.
3. Write a paper on the ethnic and racial tensions that Sinclair presents in the novel.
4. If any member of your own family emigrated in the late nineteenth or early twentieth centuries, report to the class what you find out about them, their reasons for emigrating, and their work on coming to the United States.
5. Write a paper on child labor in the early decades of the twentieth century.
6. Do a reading and careful analysis of Carl Sandburg's poem "Chicago."
7. Write a report on the career of Eugene Debs or Jack London, both of whom were important figures in Sinclair's political development.
8. Conduct a report on the legislation enacted in Franklin Roosevelt's administration that would have made life better for workers in the packing plants.
9. After meticulous research, have a debate on the following statement: "For the good of the country, capitalism should not be heavily regulated."
10. Conduct some research on the concept of the monopoly. How is it defined? What is its effect on society, commerce, and the worker? What has been the major legislation with regard to monopolies? How would you define monopolies today?
11. Make a book report on *Fast Food Nation*.

FURTHER READING

Barrett, James R. *Work and Community in the Jungle: Chicago's Packinghouse Workers, 1894–1922.* Urbana and Chicago: University of Illinois Press, 1987.

Bushnell, Charles J. *The Social Problem at the Chicago Stock Yards*. Chicago: The University of Chicago Press, 1902.

Corey, Lewis. *Meat and Man: A Study of Monopoly, Unionism, and Food Policy*. New York: Viking, 1950.

Freedman, Russell. *Kids at Work*. New York: Clarion Books, 1994.

Halpern, Rick. *Down on the Killing Floor*. Urbana and Chicago: University of Illinois Press, 1997.

Harris, Leon. *Upton Sinclair, American Rebel*. New York: 1975.

Schlosser, Eric. *Fast Food Nation: The Dark Side of the American Meal*. New York: HarperCollins, 2002.

Shannon, David A. *The Socialist Party of America*. New York: Macmillan, 1955.

Sinclair, Upton. *The Jungle*. Introduction and Notes by Maura Spiegel. New York: Barnes and Noble, 2003.

Skaggs, Jimmy M. *Prime Cut: Livestock Raising and Meatpacking in the United States, 1607–1983*. College Station, TX: Texas A&M University Press, 1986.

Slayton, Robert A. *Back of the Yards*. Chicago and London: The University of Chicago Press, 1986.

Wade, Louise Carroll. *Chicago's Pride*. Urbana and Chicago: University of Illinois Press, 1987.

7

John Steinbeck's
The Grapes of Wrath

John Steinbeck, reared in the middle of rich California farmland, immortalized the migrant farmworker in his greatest novel, *The Grapes of Wrath*. It was written and published in the 1930s and took the 1930s as its subject. The problems it raised were critical at the time of its publication and are just as timely 65 years later as they were when the book was written. The concerns of the novel include both those that are universal to workers throughout all occupations and all ages and those that were particular to farmworkers in the 1930s, including displacement; unemployment; intimidation and violence encouraged by owners in collaboration with law enforcement; poverty and starvation; lack of workers' compensation, medical care, retirement, and social services; and child labor.

The Grapes of Wrath is a product and a testament of America's greatest economic disaster in the 1930s. Widespread, unethical, reckless investing in the stock market, banking irregularities, and concentration on the production of what were then luxury items led to the collapse of financial institutions and the economic bedrock of the United States. Stocks plummeted, banks failed (leaving investors deprived of their savings), businesses folded, banks foreclosed on property and land, and millions were thrown out of work.

Between 1929 and 1932, bank customers in the United States lost $1,337,244,816 in deposits and savings. Throughout the 1930s, more than 90,000 large businesses folded, throwing their employees (about one-fourth of the labor force) out of work. A total of 15 million people were without jobs in the depression. Without jobs and unable to make payments on their mortgages, thousands of families were thrown out on the street or off their farms. The rate of displacement reached horrific levels. Families who had cars and trucks lived in their vehicles.

Hoovervilles, named for President Herbert Hoover, sprang up on the edges of cities—filthy areas where families lived in shacks made of cardboard and scrap metal. Whether in a Hooverville, a flophouse, or on a park bench, families often slept under newspapers, what were called Hoover blankets.

Those who were still able to work were frequently reduced to part time. Wages were cut drastically, and working conditions became abominable. When the government made it impossible for employers to demand excessively long hours of their workers, the response was the speed-up and stretch-out, which allowed their employers to work them twice as fast. The workers' desperation to secure and retain their jobs dampened many objections to unfair labor practices.

In urban areas, especially in the Northeast, the change from carefree abundance to economic tragedy came suddenly, but people in small towns and rural farming areas, especially in the South and Midwest, had been experiencing economic hard times for almost a decade. One of the causes of the farmworkers' distress was mechanization. New machines revolutionized farming, leading many tenant farmers without livelihoods. The diesel tractor, especially, took jobs from those who had made their livings with horse and plow. Cotton-picking machines were on the horizon in the late 1930s, threatening even more jobs.

Even before the stock market crash, farmers who had provided farm produce to Europe as well as the United States had seen their overseas markets dry up and profits plummet. The price of farm produce and the price of farmland itself declined dramatically. Cotton, which had been $.35 per pound in 1919, had fallen to $.16 per pound in 1920. Farmland, which had been worth $150 an acre in 1919, had fallen to $35 an acre five years later. Small family farms could not easily be maintained in light of continual declines in produce and land. More and more small farms were incorporated into agribusinesses run by absentee landlords. With the crash of the stock market, the cost of farm produce dropped even more. Farmers, even before the crash, had borrowed heavily to keep up their equipment and farms. When the crash occurred, the collateral they had put up for their loans (usually their farms) had become virtually worthless. After 1929, banks foreclosed on farms and auctioned them off by the thousands.

Nature also conspired to displace farmers in the south central area of the country. Farmers had suffered for years from hot, arid weather. Uncustomary heat and drought and massive dust storms all served to deplete the earth of topsoil and turn it into the equivalent of hard tile. Dust storms began in 1931, when the weather was so hot that farmers could not work during the day. Dust storms, inflicting farmers and children in their path with a sickness known as dust pneumonia, were responsible for many deaths. By 1940, one-fourth of the population had fled the Southern Plains states.

Many farmworkers in the Southern Plains states like Oklahoma were tenant farmers or sharecroppers. They did not own the farms they worked on. Their housing was either rented from or provided by the land owner. The tenant farmer paid his rent from the produce he raised. For the use of the house and land, he paid the owner with 1/2 of the harvested crops. Because both tenant farmers and sharecroppers had to borrow money from the owners to buy farm supplies and pay for the first year's expenses (until the crops came in), they were always in debt to the owner. With all members of the family working, the average income was about $200 a year, much of which had to go to pay off debts. Their living conditions were squalid, malnutrition was epidemic, and death rates were high.

As small farmers were deprived of their own land, they became tenant farmers or sharecroppers on other people's land. But the overabundance of tenants, croppers, and new technology meant that thousands of farmworkers lost their jobs. Those who were still able to farm made about $.50 per day in 1932.

The history of California farming was markedly different from that in the Southern Plains states from where the Joads came. California had never been a state primarily of small- and medium-sized family farms. Before the gold rush, Spain had deeded massive tracts of hundreds of thousands of acres to a few distinguished families. The practice continued when Mexico ruled the territory. Even with the introduction of laws intended to limit the size of land grants, mega-farms continued. In 1870 wheat farms were between 43,266 acres and 300,000 acres. There were 713 farms larger than 1,000 acres in California. In 1933, large owners of mega-farms constituted 24.6 percent of all farmland and produced 73.4 percent of harvested crops.

Labor was managed as if it was a part of a big industry instead, as it often was in the Southern Plains, like an extended family. The work was done by armies of hired hands who, because of the seasonal work, could never be a stable part of any community. In California the divide between owners (who began calling themselves "growers") and their workers was exceptionally wide. The best interests of one group became diametrically opposed to that of the other group.

In 1930 and 1931, the state paid Mexican migrant workers to return to Mexico so it would not have to pay for their social services. The result was a shortage of labor, news of which traveled far and wide, and proved hopeful, above all, to farmworkers in the Plains states and southern states. Soon California growers were issuing circulars and ads in newspapers throughout the Plains states promising work in California. They guaranteed dependable work with decent wages in a land of beauty and plenty. It had been their practice for decades to advertise for many more workers than they intended to hire. When so many more workers showed up than were hired, owners could keep wages low (during the Depression wages dropped to $.10 per hour for stoop labor, or the hard labor of planting, cultivating, and harvesting crops), living conditions shameful, and company store prices high. What were called labor contractors, who were supposed to find people jobs for a fee, were (and are) notoriously corrupt. For a time in California they were outlawed.

A senate investigation into farm labor in the 1930s, chaired by Wisconsin senator Robert La Follette, revealed some of the atrocities perpetrated by the growers. One thing La Follette found was that the average salary for a farmworker was $.15 per hour, half of what they made a decade earlier. The attitude of the growers was expressed at the hearings by Henry L. Strobel: "We had requests for higher wages at all times, but most of our agricultural workers realized at that time that they were lucky to have a job at all" (Hearings before a Subcommittee of the Committee on Education and Labor, 76th Congress, Part 53; Washington, DC: U.S. Government Printing Office, 1940).

Investigators found the migrants living in unspeakable poverty in rotten tents with polluted water running through the camps. Children were overworked, malnourished, and unschooled. In 1938, the year of the action in *The Grapes of Wrath*, torrential rains hit the agricultural valleys, and migrants, flooded out of their tents and trailer parks, were living out in the open—cold and wet under trees.

The animosity between the growers and workers grew into war. The growers and native workers saw the interlopers from Oklahoma and Kansas as threats. They charged that migrants brought disease, that they were creating disorder, even fomenting revolution. Workers, they charged, were immoral, lazy, stupid, and filthy. Vigilantes hired by the growers constantly harassed the workers that owners had been at such pains to attract. Workers were driven out of towns, their camps raided, and they were refused entry into California. In 1938, California insisted that migrants return to their native states.

The migratory nature of the workers—on the move from week to week—the cultural divisions among the workers, their starvation and utter powerlessness, and the violent and oppressive tactics of the growers made negotiating to improve wages and living conditions difficult. Still, the injustice of the growers did lead to occasional strikes and picketing. The first recorded farmworkers' strike was that of Japanese and Mexican beet workers in Oxnard, California. The strikers asked the American Federation of Labor for admission into that union but were rejected. The first group to offer aid to farmworkers was the radical Industrial Workers of the World, called the Wobblies. Though few farmworkers actually belonged to the IWW, the Wobblies began to send organizers into ranches where unrest was reported. An unorganized uprising, sparked by appalling conditions, occurred in 1913 on the Wheatland Ranch owned by Ralph Durst. For instance, Durst provided no drinking water in the fields. The workers' only recourse was to buy lemonade, made solely of chemicals, from Durst's brother. The Wobblies moved in to assist the workers, but Durst brought in state and local law enforcement, resulting in four deaths and hundreds of injuries. In 1930 there was another effort at organizing farmworkers. The most effective union was the Cannery and Agricultural Workers' Industrial Union, which presented the following demands on behalf of farmworkers: $.75 per hour for skilled labor, time and a half for overtime, decent housing and sanitation, abolition of child labor, equal pay for men and women, and pay by the hour. In 1933, in the Central Valley, 20,000 cotton workers struck. Many other independent strikes arose in the early 1930s but without any gains for the workers. Their leaders were inevitably rooted out, beaten savagely, and sometimes killed. Other picketers and strikers were fired and blacklisted.

THE STORY OF THE JOADS

The classic story of the Joads, associated in the general consciousness with their experiences in California, is actually divided into three major parts. Chapters 1–11 are set in Oklahoma; Chapters 11–18 are about the trip to California. Only the last 12 chapters, 18–30, take place in California.

The story begins with young Tom Joad, who is walking and hitchhiking home after having served time in an Oklahoma prison for killing a man in self-defense during a drunken brawl. Released on parole, he is on his way to his family, who once owned their own land but have been sharecroppers for generations. On his way, he is joined by Jim Casy, a family friend and former country preacher now turned religious seeker. As they approach the family house, they see that it is deserted and in ruins, but another farmer in the general area informs them of the family's whereabouts: They have been displaced and are living with Tom's Uncle John.

When Tom and Casy reach the house, Pa Joad is loading a truck in preparation for a move to California. The family consists of Ma and Pa, Granma and Grampa, Tom's grown siblings—Noah, Al, and Rose of Sharon, who is now married and pregnant—and two young children, Ruthie and Winfield. In addition, Uncle John, Rose of Sharon's husband Connie, and eventually Jim Casy make up the party heading west.

Tom learns that the family has been thrown off the land or tractored out, as have 100,000 other farming families. The Joads are loading up their truck with possessions that they cannot take and need to be sold. For these tools and other things, they receive a pittance, just one of many cases in which businesspeople cheated the farmers going west. The Joads and other farmers cling to the idea of California as Eden—a place of plentiful food, sunshine, and, most of all, jobs. Their ideal is presented as a little white house surrounded by orange trees. Although Tom also looks forward to work in California, he has gotten wind of the low wages, unemployment, and dirty camps to be found there. And Tom faces another impediment that he decides to ignore: He will be breaking parole if he crosses out of Oklahoma.

They pack the truck; then they slaughter, butcher, cook, and salt down two pigs to take along. Their only trouble is the feisty Grampa, who at the last minute refuses to go, forcing them to drug him to get him on the truck to leave. Then they join the army of farmers heading down Highway 66 toward California. Always apprehensive about running out of water or gasoline or having a breakdown, and occasionally admitting the nagging fear that there will not be work in California, they still move forward in hope toward the dream of work and a decent life.

In the evening, looking for a place to stop and spend the night, they spot a couple who have pulled off the road into a protected clearing. Ivy Wilson and his sick wife Sairy welcome them, inviting them to place the dying Grampa in the Wilson tent. After Grampa dies (Casy says he actually died when he was taken off the land), the men dig a grave at night and bury him. In return for the Wilsons' kindness, Al fixes their car and the Joad family invites the Wilsons to travel with them.

On the road for a brief time, another disaster occurs when the truck breaks down. Al, Casy, and Tom take the family to a private camp up the road, go into town for parts, and return to fix the car. While the car can be fixed, Granma cannot. The family has to acknowledge that she has completely lost her mind.

In the private camp, they meet a ragged man returning to Oklahoma who reports on the gruesome situation in California, where his wife and children have died of starvation. They are forced by the unpleasant camp owner to move out, and they head for the Arizona border. They cross the driest of deserts in getting to California and stop by a river where the men in the Joad family relax in the water with other travelers. Here they meet another man and his son returning from California. They offer further details of poverty and police brutality, asserting that there are 300,000 so-called Okies in California living like hogs and hated.

In the evening, Tom has to report to the family that Noah has departed, making his way up the river on his own. Before they can settle in to rest in the riverside camp, however, police move them on, telling them they are not wanted. The Joads ready the truck to move out, but the Wilsons regretfully announce their decision to stay. Sairy is too sick to move on. With the worst of the desert before them, Ma worries that Granma, the pregnant Rose of Sharon, and the two young children will not have enough water. At another inspection point, officers insist on examining their belongings for contraband plants and fruits, but Ma boldly inter-cepts and adamantly refuses to let them examine the truck. The inspec-tors relent and pass them through, whereupon Ma informs the family that Granma has died. She was terrified that, if the officers had found the dead body, they would have refused to allow the family to proceed.

They leave Granma's body at the coroner's office outside town and find a Hooverville to camp in. Tom befriends a man named Floyd, who informs them that there is no work in the area and warns him that the growers and contractors will cheat them however they can. When a labor contractor drives up at night to offer work, Floyd challenges him to put his offer, including a salary, in writing. This prompts an armed deputy to emerge from the car to arrest Floyd as a troublemaker. Floyd gets away by attacking the man and running into the willows while the deputy reck-lessly fires at him, seriously injuring a woman in a tent. But Tom trips the deputy and Casy kicks him in the throat. Tom is told to hide; numerous armed men return; and Casy offers himself as the real attacker.

The family decides to move south before deputies return to burn out the camp, as they inevitably will. Before they leave, they must come to terms with the fact that Connie, Rose of Sharon's husband, has deserted her. They must also find Uncle John, who has gone on one of his infrequent binges. Tom, who has returned from hiding, finds a resistant Uncle John, knocks him out, and carries him to the departing truck.

Their destination is Weedpatch, a government camp that has been recommended to them. For the Joads, Weedpatch is an ideal community under the circumstances. It has toilets and showers, laundry facilities, play areas, medical care, entertainment, and, most of all, self-government. Growers resent the government camps because workers expect the same decent conditions in company camps—things that would cost the growers money. Companies also despise the self-government of the camps, fearing that cooperation will lead to union organizing. So growers hire the assistance of law enforcement to shut down camps. But their underhanded attack on Weedpatch fails.

Despite the pleasant atmosphere, however, after a month, the only work they have gotten is Tom's five days digging a pipeline for $.25 an hour. Moreover, they find that wages are going down even farther for those few who have succeeded in finding work. At Ma's insistence, they leave Weedpatch to find work farther up north and, on the same day, come across a man promising work near Pixley. Their suspicions are aroused when the long line of cars of families seeking work is escorted by police, and they ride through lines of men on the side of the road, who are shouting angrily and carrying signs.

The Hooper ranch is like a fortress. They are ushered into the camp of 50 one-room, boxlike houses with one window and one door—filthy, dilapidated structures where grease runs down the walls and that are furnished only with a rusty stove. An armed guard is stationed at each end of each row of houses. Workers find that they will be paid $.05 per box for picked peaches. It finally dawns on them that they are unwitting scabs. On an evening stroll, Tom finds that they are locked inside the camp and overhears guards making plans to find and kill the strike leader. But Tom is able to sneak out under a fence and quickly stumbles on a tent where the strike leaders are hiding. There he is reunited with Jim Casy, who has become the strike leader.

Tom learns from Casy that the wages of the striking workers had been dropped to $.025 a box; scabs were now receiving $.05, but when the strike is broken, the price will again drop to $.025. In the middle of Tom's talk with Casy, company vigilantes surround the tent and kill Casy. Tom slams the murderer with a pick handle, almost certainly killing him, and then is himself hit across the face and badly wounded.

Posses begin looking for Tom, who now poses a danger to his family. They also learn that with the death of Casy and the subsequent breaking of the strike, wages have indeed dropped to $.025 per box. The Joads hide Tom in the back of the truck and leave. Near a camp of boxcars where they hope to pick cotton, Tom leaves the family and hides in the underbrush until his face heals. In a fight in the boxcar camp, his little sister, Ruthie, brags that her brother has killed two men and is hiding, so Tom has to leave the area, vowing to carry on Casy's cause. The Joad men only find a half a day's work picking cotton.

Then the rains come. As Pa and other men spend all day making an embankment that a tree eventually tears down on the same day, Rose of Sharon delivers a stillborn baby. The water floods the truck and rises inch by inch in the boxcar where they live. Uncle John, who has been given the box containing the dead baby, takes it to a river and lowers it in, saying that the baby will float into town where it will speak for all the desperate farmworkers. Finally, seeking dry, higher ground, Pa wades through the high water carrying Rose of Sharon on his back. He and the remaining Joad family spot an abandoned barn on dry ground, where they go for shelter. Here they encounter a young boy and his father, dying of starvation and too weak to consume solid food. The narrative ends with Rose of Sharon feeding the stranger with her own mother's milk, intended for the infant who was born dead.

LABOR ISSUES

Interspersed throughout the narrative of the Joads' journey are chapters serving as commentaries on the issues facing the agricultural laborers of the 1930s:

Chapter 1: The dust storms ravage the plains farms.
Chapter 5: The depleted land and the introduction of the tractor forces foreclosures and displacements.
Chapter 7: The desperate farmers, displaced and needing to move to find work, are cheated by merchants, including car salesmen.
Chapter 9: They are also cheated by merchants to whom they must sell the possessions they are to leave behind
Chapter 11: One man on a tractor takes the place of 12–17 families, and he plows through houses, barns, hills, and gullies.
Chapter 12: On Highway 66, the road of flight, families fear taking their rickety car over high mountains and deserts without

adequate supplies. They fear border patrols and are cheated by gas station owners.

Chapter 14: The damage done by banks and tractors leads to anger and unrest.

Chapter 17: A code of honor develops in camps along the way among people lured to California and hoping to find work.

Chapter 19: California's vast lands are in the hands of too few people, who join together to exploit migrant workers.

Chapter 21: Big landowners buy canneries, sell their produce at rock-bottom prices to their own canneries, and thereby drive small farmers out of business and maintain low wages and inflated prices.

Chapter 23: Workers escape their misery by sharing stories, singing, dancing, drinking, and immersing themselves in religion.

Chapter 25: To drive up the price of farm produce, oranges are dumped and soaked in kerosene, guards keep starving people from fishing potatoes out of the river where they have been dumped, livestock is slaughtered and buried, and milk is poured into streams.

Chapter 27: Men pick cotton, one of the major stoop crops, for $.80 per hundred pounds, and their bags are weighed by the growers on crooked scales.

Chapter 29: When the torrential rains begin in California, water rises in fields, tents, and cabins, and there is no social relief for people who are starving and sick, and have been out of work for months.

UNEMPLOYMENT

The most distressing labor issue raised by *The Grapes of Wrath*, from which other problems derive, is society's refusal of work to the worker. Looking at the Oklahoma part of the story, one sees that numerous conditions have come together to deny small farmers and farm laborers the work necessary for them to support their families. A truck driver first alerts Tom to the situation he will find when he reaches home. The men, thrown out of work because they have been thrown off the land, ponder the philosophical question of who owns the land. Is it the legal owner or the bank with a piece of paper? Or is it the person who has actually, daily, year after year, labored on the soil, who has mixed his labor with the land, whose family is buried on the land, and whose children have been reared on it? In short, what constitutes ownership? Capital or labor?

Sure, cried the tenant men, but it's our land. We measured it and broke it up. We were born on it, and we got killed on it, died on it. Even if it's no good, it's still ours. That's what makes it ours—being born on it, working it, dying on it. That makes ownership, not a paper with numbers on it. (Steinbeck 45)

The Joads have been wrenched away from something that is a vital part of them. No wonder Casy says that Grampa died the moment he was forced off the home place. Moreover, a person's labor is an essential part of who he or she is. In taking away their opportunity to labor and refusing to provide them with other labor, society has unmanned them. On more than one occasion, the farmworkers in *The Grapes of Wrath* observe that when a horse on a ranch has no work (in the rainy season, for example), it is still fed and cared for. But when a human worker has no work, he is thrown out to starve.

Because of the seasonal nature of the work, the agricultural workers are forced to become migrants. Because they can never live in one place long enough to establish residency, they are unable to obtain the meager social services that were available in the 1930s, before the development of President Franklin Roosevelt's New Deal.

WORK AND WAGES

Even for those who do find work, the working and living conditions are inhumane. With work of any kind so hard to secure, owners can get by with paying poverty-level wages. About the time the Joads arrive in California, the growers association has dropped the standard wage of $.30 per hour to $.25 per hour. And Tom finds out at the Hooverville just after they arrive that, in reality, some of the owners are paying as little as $.15 per hour, and wages are going down even further. At the Hooper ranch, pay has dropped from $.05 per crate to $.025 per crate. After they leave the Hooper ranch, they are employed as cotton pickers and are paid $.80–.90 per hundred pounds. The most they make a day is $3.00.

They have their first real experience of picking fruit on the Hooper ranch. All members of the family, including Ma and the two young children, help to fill the box with peaches. After the crop is picked, of course, there will be no work. Workers fight over the trees so they can fill their buckets faster. Each bucket holds three gallons of peaches, and each box holds nine gallons. It is for this nine-gallon box that they are paid $.025–.05. The first box Tom presents for his nickel is rejected because he has bruised the fruit.

After working most of a day in the hot sun, the family has picked 20 boxes, or 180 gallons of peaches. At the scab rate of $.05 per box, they have made one dollar. The next day they make $1.42. Even then, they are not paid in cash, but in company scrip, which can only be used at the company store, where the price of all the goods has been inflated.

The cotton crop is also seasonal, so farmworkers fight over the rows here as well. Pickers are charged one dollar for the bags they need to pick cotton. It is stoop work that ruins the laborers' backs. On top of that, the bags become extremely heavy and must be pulled along the ground.

ABROGATION OF WORKERS' RIGHTS

The agricultural workers in *The Grapes of Wrath* live in a police state, in which the growers band together to make the greatest possible profit by spending the least amount of money to harvest their crops. To do this, they advertise for armies of workers who are desperate for work and will even work for food. The growers then expend the least amount of money on the camps where their workers must live. Realizing that they are creating conditions for rebellion, growers buy law enforcement officers—state troopers, local deputies, and private vigilantes—to intimidate workers, especially those who might pose a threat of organizing strikes. The growers' reaction to what they sense is rising anger is to urge more violence against them. Anyone who complains is labeled a "Red," or communist.

The Joads get some advance word of this situation in a camp along the way from a man returning from California. He warns them that deputies push farmers around and that if they dare pick an orange to eat, they will be shot. Soon they have their own experience with the growers' and labor contractors' lawmen when a man with a badge and a gun orders them out of a camp. "'If you're here tomorra this time I'll run you in. We don't want none of you settlin' down here'" (291).

At the next camp site in a Hooverville, they are told that deputies burn out the camps periodically so the workers will not stay long enough to be qualified to vote or get welfare assistance. In their first Hooverville, they are attacked by a labor contractor and his armed escort, who shoots recklessly into the camp, severing the finger of a woman in her tent. Floyd tells Tom that it does no good to organize, picket, or strike because the owners inevitably have the leaders arrested, beaten, ordered out of the area, and blacklisted. Jim Casy meets an even worse fate as he is hunted down and killed for organizing the strike against the Hooper Ranch.

AFTER *THE GRAPES OF WRATH*

Ironically, it was World War II that saved many of the Southern Plains farmworkers who had come to California to work in the fields, for it was the growth of the defense industry that finally provided them with jobs. As these families left the fields, they were replaced by Mexican and Central American workers who entered California to take their place. But federal legislation, designed to help labor in general, did not apply to farmworkers and, even though California passed its own laws to help farmworkers, wages and living and working conditions continued to be abominable.

Because of a shortage of workers during the war, growers instituted the Bracero program, which allowed them to import young Mexican workers to complete specific jobs before being returned to their home country. Growers preferred the Bracero program because the young people did not place demands on them for decent living and working conditions, did not join unions, and could be immediately deported if they caused problems.

Old problems persisted and new problems arose after World War II. For example, farmworkers for the first time were being exposed to pesticides, and growers used a labor union, the Teamsters, to threaten and beat complaining farmworkers. But farmworkers began to organize into unions and negotiate for improvements in their conditions after the war. The longest strike to date, from 1947 to 1950, was organized by Ernesto Galarza of the National Farm Labor Union against one of the larger growers, the DiGiorgio Fruit Corporation. The union asked for a raise of $.10 per hour and a way to air their grievances. The strike failed in 1950 after the strike leaders were fired and picketers were seriously wounded.

Finally, in the 1960s, Cesar Chavez rose to greatness as a leader of agricultural workers with the establishment of the United Farm Workers. In 1965, a strike was organized against growers of table grapes and national pleas were issued to boycott grapes, and later, lettuce. After five years, an agreement was reached between the union and grape-growing corporations. The growers agreed to a $.15-per-hour raise; to an additional $.12 per hour for health and welfare benefits; to hire from the union halls rather than from labor contractors; to monitor pesticides; and to allow workers to elect their own representatives. The union fought for and secured benefits for farmworkers throughout Chavez's lifetime. He died in 1993.

FARMWORKERS TODAY

Unfortunately, the living and working conditions of farmworkers have gone steadily downhill in the twenty-first century. Federal protections afforded other workers are still not available to agricultural workers. Franklin Roosevelt's National Labor Relations Act and the Fair Labor Standards Act (FSLA), which regulated wages, overtime, and child labor, had no bearing on farm labor which was exempt from both laws. When the FLSA was amended in 1966 to cover farmworkers, it still exempted farms hiring 500 men or fewer. Farmworkers were also unable to benefit from legislation guaranteeing pensions, unemployment, and workers' compensation

Like all workers in the 1930s, wage earners in the United States today face massive unemployment in all sectors of the economy. In sheer numbers, unemployment in 2004 is the worst since the 1930s, under Herbert Hoover, during the Great Depression. From 2001 to 2004, the number of jobs lost in the private sector was 2,931,000. The total number of unemployed Americans in this period reached 8,170,000. Those who remain unemployed for more than a month are unaccounted for in the Bureau of Labor Statistics. Another situation that government statistics fail to take into account is that many who lost their jobs were only able to find work at significantly lower-paying jobs.

Unemployment, specifically among farmworkers, is especially high, in part because of the large numbers of people seeking farmwork. Like the Okies of the 1930s, the people who harvest our food in California, Florida, Washington State, North Carolina, and elsewhere have uprooted themselves to escape the poverty of their native land. Statistics for 2004 found that only 14 percent of all farmworkers had fulltime employment, and that 39,000 farmworkers did not receive wages. As with the case of the Joads working in the peach orchards, children and other family members work only to help the main breadwinners fill their quotas of picked fruit.

In many farms throughout the United States, agricultural workers face an unspeakable, inhumane condition undreamed of by the Joads. A case in point is the shocking number of workers who are literally enslaved on farms. They are not allowed to leave and are paid no wages. The Joads experienced a brief episode of something like slavery on the Hooper Ranch, where workers were locked in the housing compound at night, but there is nothing in *The Grapes of Wrath* to compare with the enslavement of farmworkers today. Since 1996, six owners have been convicted for enslaving workers against their will. The most notorious involved a Florida owner's enslavement of hundreds of workers, coerced into working without pay. They were told that if they dared to try to escape, their tongues would be cut off. Those who work as advocates for farmworkers suspect that there are many more cases of enslavement of farmworkers that remain hidden. An Associated Press article appearing in the *West County Times* declared that there were more than 16,000 cases of slavery in the United States each year ("Migrant Smuggling Said to Breed Slavery," May 3, 2005, p. A15).

The June 11, 2005, *New York Times* ran an article on another case of enslaved farmworkers that has come to light in East Palatka, Florida, a potato and cabbage growing area. This case is different from the usual cases of farmworker enslavement in that the workers are not illegal immigrants, allowing themselves to become enslaved for fear of being turned over to the authorities. In this case, the workers have been born in the United States. They are homeless and African American, and most of them are addicted to drugs or alcohol. The farm labor contractor and his assistants have been charged with luring people with the promise of work, room, and board. At the end of the workday, cigarettes, alcohol, and crack cocaine are provided to them, deducted from their pay, which is inadequate to meet these expenses and so is given on credit. Shortly, the laborers run up massive debts to the owners and contractors who use force to retain them as slaves (A10).

Even without considering the cases of enslavement, it is generally agreed that the gains won for farmworkers by Cesar Chavez in the 1970s have largely been lost now. The wages of farmworkers are increasingly well below the poverty line. In 1990, 50 percent of farmworkers lived below the poverty line; by 1995, this had risen to 60 percent. In 2005, the average annual wage reported for a farmworker is $7,500 a year or about $6.14 an hour, the lowest of all workers in the United States. Yet even this figure is inflated. Advocates claim that the method of reporting misrepresents a much lower hourly wage; it has been gauged on an 8-hour day, when in fact, laborers are working 12–14 hours a day. Small farms employing 500 workers or fewer are exempt from paying the minimum wage. Because of the surplus of labor, owners have been able to sharply reduce pay every year in the last two decades of the twentieth century. For example, in 1980, workers had to pick 7 buckets of tomatoes a day to earn a minimum wage. But in 2005, workers must pick between 100 and 150 buckets of tomatoes to earn $40 per day. At the same time that wages have gone down, prices have gone up.

References to the greed of corporate owners in *The Grapes of Wrath* make today's corporate profits pertinent to this discussion. The average wage for farmworkers in 2003 was $7,500 a year; at the same time, in one year, the chief executive officer of the world's leading producer of soy meal, corn, wheat, and cocoa, received $2.9 *million* dollars. The Dole Company, the largest producer of fruits, vegetables, and flowers, made a $4.8 *billion* dollar profit in 2003. Profits reaped by agribusinesses have continued to be among the highest in the United States.

Working conditions of farm laborers are in many ways as poor as they were in the 1930s and, in many instances, worse. Work in the fields has become one of the most perilous of occupations, second only to mining. Much of the labor is stoop labor, which requires the worker to bend over constantly to pick low-growing crops. The chief physical complaints are of pain and sprains of the back, shoulders, arms, and hands. Legislation was enacted in some areas to force growers to provide long-handled hoes instead of short ones that require the worker to bend down, but growers have managed to get around the law to insist on short hoes. In addition, the farmworker must lift and carry extremely heavy loads of produce.

The intense heat in the fields poses a deadly danger to workers. On August 22, 2004, Juliana Barbassa reported the situation in an article headlined "Heat Stroke Poses Ever-Present Farmworker Peril" (*The West County Times*, Contra Costa County, California, A6). Her subject was the death of a grape picker, 53-year-old Asuncion Valdivia, on July 28, 2004, in Bakersfield, California. To provide an idea of the extent of the problem, four workers were on record as having died from heatstroke in 1998 and three in 2002. In 1992 (the last year for which complete statistics are available), 41 farmworkers were hospitalized for more than 24 hours with heat stroke. For those who do not go to hospitals or are hospitalized for less than 24 hours, there are no records. Conditions are especially dangerous for grape pickers in the Central Valley, where temperatures reach 100 degrees. Workers are paid by the box, weighing from 23 to 26 pounds, and because the grapes must be picked within a short period of time, workers are expected to produce from 40 to 50 boxes a day. Thus, the speed with which they must work contributes to exhaustion and injuries. Valdivia's case illustrates the problem. When he collapsed in the field, he had been picking fruit at top speed for 10 hours in intense heat, over 100 degrees. His fellow workers were unsure of what was wrong with him or what the best course of action might be, and their supervisor was unresponsive. The ambulance someone called never came, because it was cancelled by the foreman. Valdivia's son was expected to drive his father home in a vehicle without air conditioning. When they finally reached the hospital, the dying worker's body temperature was 108 degrees.

Many deaths have also been reported of workers having to enter manure pits maintained on farms for fertilizer. One of the worst cases occurred in 1989, when five farmworkers died after being asphyxiated by poisonous fumes emitted from a manure pit they entered on a dairy farm.

One of the greatest dangers facing workers in the fields today is the exposure to pesticides. The Environmental Protection Agency estimates that some 300,000 laborers are poisoned by exposure to pesticides each year. Often this poison reaches workers in the field from crop dusting, which invariably blows pesticides in areas off the target. Sometimes workers are immediately sickened, and sometimes the poison works more slowly and insidiously. In 1989, Cesar Chavez warned of this danger, indicating that in the area of McFarland, a farm town near the grape-growing area of Delano, California, the rate of cancer was 400 percent above normal. In 1996, the immediate effects of pesticides from crop dusting became shockingly apparent when 22 farmworkers had to be rushed to the hospital and another 225 people were sickened by exposure to deadly chemicals blown across the fields in which they were working. In California in 2002, it is estimated that 1,316 people showed the ill effects of pesticides. And in May 2004, another crew of 19 farmworkers began suffering nausea, losing consciousness, and having blurry vision after exposure to pesticides in the fields.

Today, in California, where the Joads lived, the rate of work-related illness and injury among farmworkers is three times that of the population as a whole, and the death rate for farmworkers is five times that of other laborers. The life expectancy of farmworkers is 25 years below the national average.

The living conditions in company camps are still atrocious. Of the growers who submitted to water testing in North Carolina, 44 percent had contaminated water. In 1986, 86 percent of workers tested suffered from the effects of contaminated water. Company housing consists of shabby trailers, sheds, garages, and shared motel rooms. They usually lack plumbing and appliances.

One of the most recent articles, which appeared shortly before this volume went to press, is titled "A Side Order of Human Rights" (*The New York Times*, April 6, 2005, p. A29). The writer, Eric Schlosser, author of *Fast Food Nation*, was prompted to address the problems of farmworkers when a four-year boycott of Taco Bell in Florida ended with Taco Bell's acceding to the workers' demands in March 2005. The workers wanted an increase in wages, decent conduct on the part of suppliers, the end of indentured servitude and slavery. Taco Bell finally agreed to pay a penny more per pound for tomatoes to suppliers who would pass the raise along to pickers in wages.

In summary, farmworkers have had and continue to have occasional small victories in their struggle for a decent life, but the lives of those who reap the crops that the country requires and enjoys are as squalid and dehumanizing today as they were when John Steinbeck published *The Grapes of Wrath*.

QUESTIONS AND PROJECTS

1. Write a feature article, based on extensive research, about the farm products produced near you or in your state. Make a visit to a large farm part of your project.
2. Make a report on agricultural laborers who either work near you or somewhere in your state. If you find that migrant labor is used, include them in your project.
3. Write a separate report on the history of child labor in the fields, bringing it up to the present time.
4. Preferably using a series of interviews, research the question of communities' attitudes toward migrant workers. Compare it with that shown in *The Grapes of Wrath*.
5. Write a detailed history of Cesar Chavez's work to improve the condition of farmworkers.
6. Imagine that the Joads are arrested for trespassing and stealing food. Stage a drama in the form of a trial in which a grower and Pa Joad clash over basic issues touching workers.
7. The debate continues in the twenty-first century between those who think government owes protection to employees and those who think government is too big and interference will hurt business and, thus, the nation. Formulate a question along these lines to debate in class.
8. Write and perform an evening of narrative and Woody Guthrie's songs, pertinent to *The Grapes of Wrath*.

FURTHER READING

Bernstein, Irving. *Turbulent Years: A History of the American Worker, 1933–1941*. Boston: Houghton Mifflin, 1970.

Cletus, Daniel E. *Bitter Harvest: A History of California Farmworkers.* Berkeley, CA: University of California Press, 1981.

Cross, William T. and Dorothy Cross. *Newcomers and Nomads in California.* Palo Alto, CA: Stanford University Press, 1937.

Ditsky, John. *Critical Essays on Steinbeck's* The Grapes of Wrath. Boston: G.K. Hall, 1989.

Ferris, Susan, and Ricardo Sandoval. *The Fight in the Fields.* New York: Harcourt Brace and Co., 1997.

Gregory, James. *American Exodus: The Dust Bowl Migration and Okie Culture in California.* New York: Oxford University Press, 1989.

Jamieson, Stuart. *Labor Unionism in American Agriculture.* Bulletin no. 326. Washington, DC: United States Labor Statistics, 1945.

Johnson, Claudia Durst. *Understanding* The Grapes of Wrath. Westport, CT: Greenwood Press, 1999.

Loftis, Anne. *Witness to the Struggle: Imagining the 1930s California Labor Movement.* Reno, NV: University of Nevada Press, 1998.

——— and Dick Meister. *A Long Time Coming: The Struggle to Unionize America's Farmworkers.* New York: Macmillan Publishing Co, 1977.

London, Joan, and Henry Anderson. *So Shall Ye Reap.* New York: Thomas Y. Crowell, 1970.

McWilliams, Carey. *Factories in the Fields.* Boston: Little, Brown, 1942

Stein, Walter. *California and the Dust Bowl Migration.* Westport, CT: Greenwood Press, 1973.

Steinbeck, John. *In Dubious Battle.* New York: Penguin Books, 1936.

———. *The Grapes of Wrath.* New York: Penguin, 1976.

Taylor, Paul S. *On the Ground in the Thirties.* Salt Lake City, UT: Peregrine Smith, 1983.

Wyatt, David, ed. *New Essays on* The Grapes of Wrath. Cambridge: Cambridge University Press, 1990.

8

Studs Terkel's *Working*

In 1972, Studs Terkel, a Chicago-based writer and radio journalist, published what has often been referred to as a documentary masterpiece, titled *Working: People Talk about What They Do and How They Feel about What They Do.* The book is composed of Terkel's 133 interviews with a wide variety of working people. Terkel indicates in his introduction that the only well-known categories of workers he did not include were clergymen, doctors, politicians, journalists, and writers. Guided in part by Terkel, the workers he interviewed refer to the economic circumstances in which they grew up, describe the actual day-to-day work they do, their relationships with their fellow workers and bosses, the hazards of the job, their aspirations, the physical and psychological toll work takes, the moral issues involved in what they do, the status (both on and off the job) of what they perform, and their philosophical view of what they do. Although many described the hours expected of them and the pensions they can look forward to, surprisingly few make an issue of their wages or unions.

THE PLAN OF TERKEL'S BOOK

Studs Terkel's extensive and insightful introduction draws conclusions about the common threads running through the interviews. Three "Prefaces" follow the introduction. The first is a long interview with a 37-year-old steelworker, who sets up the problem of who really is responsible for building the structures of civilization throughout history. The second is composed of interviews with three young news carriers, ages 12 years, 12 years, and 14 years, who are just beginning their work lives. The third preface is an interview with a 57-year-old mason who has worked with pride at his historic trade for 40 years.

The volume is divided into nine books, covering the following:

Book One
  "Working the Land"
  Six interviews with farmers, miners, and a heavy equipmentoperator

Book Two
  "Communications"
  Interviews with a receptionist, a hotel switchboard operator, a telephone operator, and a professor of communications.
  "A Pecking Order"
  Five interviews with women: a stewardess, an airline reservationist, a model, a secretary, and a prostitute
  "Did You Ever Hear the One About the Farmer's Daughter?"
  A single interview with a script supervisor and producer for an ad agency
  "The Commercial"
  Interviews with a copy chief, two actors, a press agent, a salesman and installment dealer, and a telephone solicitor

Book Three
  "Cleaning Up"
  Interview with a garbage truck driver, a garbage collector, a washroom attendant, a factory mechanic, a domestic cleaning woman, and a janitor
  "Watching"
  Interviews with a doorman, two police officers, an industrial investigator, a photographer, and a film critic

Book Four
  "The Making"
  Interviews with two spot welders, a utility man, a stock chaser, a plant manager, a general foreman, and the president of a local union
  "The Driving"
  Interviews with two cabdrivers, a bus driver, and a truck driver
  "The Parking"
  Interview with a car hiker

"The Selling"
Interview with a car salesman

Book Five
"Appearance"
Interviews with a barber, two hairstylists, a cosmetics saleswoman, a dentist, a hotel clerk, a bar pianist, an elevator starter, and a salesman turned janitor
"Counting"
Interviews with a bank teller and an auditor
"Footwork"
Interviews with an organizer, an order filler, a mail carrier, a gas meter reader, a supermarket box boy, a supermarket checker, a skycap, a felter in a luggage factor, and a waitress
"Just a Housewife"
Interviews with two housewives

Book Six
"The Quiet Life"
Interviews with a bookbinder, a pharmacist, and a piano tuner
"Brokers"
Interviews with a real estate broker, a yacht broker, and two stock-brokers
"Bureaucracy"
Interviews with a project coordinator, a government relations coordinator, and a process clerk
"Organizer"
An interview with a labor organizer

Book Seven
"The Sporting Life"
Interviews with a jockey, a baseball player, a sports press agent, a tennis player, a hockey player, and a football coach
"In Charge"
Interviews with a radio executive, a factory owner, an audit department head in a bank, an ex-boss of a merchandize company and his daughter, and the ex-president of a conglomerate
"Ma and Pa Courage"
Interviews with two neighborhood merchants
"Reflections on Idleness and Retirement"
Interviews with a nonworking woman, who has an independent income, and two retired workers

Book Eight
   "The Age of Charlie Blossom"
      Interviews with a copy boy, a publisher, a proofreader, a salesman,
         a jazz musician, an executive, a director of a bakery cooperative,
         and a hospital aide
   "Cradle to the Grave"
      Interviews with a baby nurse, two school teachers, an occupational
         therapist, a patient's representative, a nurse in a home for the
         elderly, a memorial counselor, and a gravedigger

Book Nine
   "The Quiz Kid and the Carpenter"
      Interviews with a tree nursery worker and a carpenter
   "In Search of a Calling"
      Interviews with an editor, an industrial designer, and a social activ-
         ist who has worked at several jobs
   "Second Chance"
      Interviews with a salesman turned farmer, a lawyer, a librarian, and
         a stonecutter.
   "Fathers and Sons"
      Interviews with father and son service station owners; a steelworker
         and his son, who is a priest; a teacher; and a freight elevator
         operator and his sons, who are a police officer and a firefighter

REBELLIOUS TIMES

The years covered by Studs Terkel in *Working*—the late 1960s and
early 1970s—constitute a period of the greatest social turbulence that
the United States has ever seen. The largest political upheavals came
in the areas of civil rights, feminism, and the antiwar movement,
prompted by U.S. involvement in Vietnam. Multiple revolutions, both
large and small, affected the entire population's stance toward authority
of many kinds, whether it was the authority of individuals, institutions,
or traditional ideas.

In the Civil Rights Movement, vocational equality of opportunity for
African Americans was an important by-product of the drive for voting
rights and integration, set into motion by the 1954 U.S. Supreme Court
decision *Brown v. Board of Education,* which struck down public school
segregation. One memorable challenge to authority (as invested in local
and state government and traditions of inequality) came in 1955 when a

single woman, a weary seamstress named Rosa Parks, refused to give up her seat to a white man on a Montgomery, Alabama, city bus. Her courageous challenge of the status quo sparked a bus boycott, leading to much-needed reforms. In the middle of the boycott, another woman, Autherine Lucy, challenged the century-old authority of segregation and inequality by being admitted to the University of Alabama. She was expelled before the semester was over, on the grounds that her presence threatened the campus with violence, but her painful confrontation with authority, like that of Rosa Parks, broke racial chains and would lead to fundamental reforms. Another notable challenge to the tradition of segregation came in 1960 in Greensboro, North Carolina, where students at the local black college began sit-ins at the Woolworth's lunch counter, which, like all restaurants in the south, served only whites. In the same year, "Freedom Riders," black and white social activists from the north, came south to challenge segregation and to aid in voter registration.

The work situation of the African American was affected by the collapse of farming and the introduction of the mechanical cotton picker, leading to the dislocation of black as well as white workers in the twentieth century. Up until midcentury, the large majority of African American men and women had little opportunity for training that would admit them to trades and professions. Moreover, even if the training were available to them, they were barred from most trades, professions, and unions. The one professional role which African American men were free to assume was that of clergypersons in African American churches. The one profession available to a few African American women was school teaching. Most African Americans filled the most menial positions of garbage collectors and house cleaners. In the textile industry, for example, African Americans were barred from jobs within the factory itself. They were also specifically barred from serving as police officers and firefighters. In 1964, 1965, and 1968, civil rights legislation was passed, prompting the dismantling of segregation and the slow opening up to African Americans of education, vocational training, trades, and professions. These years were marked by the non-violent protests, led by Martin Luther King as well as violent riots in northern slums over escalating police brutality and inescapable poverty.

Another revolution was occurring among the nation's women, partly inspired by the Civil Rights Movement. Feminists taught that men and women should enjoy equal civil rights and urged the opening up of professions and trades to women. Throughout history, poor women had labored in textile factories, in mines, and on farms, performing work every bit as arduous as that of men. They managed the finances of complex entities like farms and households, and they were in the forefront of union organizing. In the 1950s, 1960s, and 1970s, women came to realize more and more that when their work was needed, as in World War II, for example, they were well regarded as being as capable of men in every part of the workforce —proven by the archetypical Rosie the Riveter. But when they were no longer needed, they lost well-paid positions, poor women returning to physically difficult, low-paying positions in industry and on farms. Forty percent of the workforce in 1969 was composed of women, but they were largely barred from management and relegated to "women's work"—child care, domestic work, elementary school teaching, nursing, waiting on tables, performing clerical work, and selling women's clothing in stores. Out of general discontent and humiliation, from being barred from professional schools and well-paying jobs, came the feminist movement, resulting, among other things, in a 1967 executive order banning sex discrimination in federal employment.

The other big social-political movement in the period of Terkel's interviews involved large-scale protests against the war in Vietnam, which lasted from 1964 to 1972. Many, including members of Congress, began questioning the reason for U.S. involvement. Deaths of U.S. soldiers in the war climbed astronomically. Reports of massacres on the part of U.S. forces also began reaching the United States. With the leadership in both political parties refusing to take seriously the need to withdraw from Vietnam, the country appeared to many in the late 1960s to be on the edge of revolution. Protests against the war were the most widespread and significant challenges to governmental authority the United States had ever seen. In 1969, for example, 100,000 people gathered on the Boston Common to protest the war. In 1971, in Washington, DC, 20,000 people protested against the war. Other protests of the same magnitude occurred throughout U.S. cities. In 1969–1970, there were more than 1,785 protests by students alone.

Moreover, there were other protests building in the United States: against the country's shameful treatment of Native Americans, against large corporations, against militarism in general, and against the pollution of the environment and the depletion of our natural resources. Numerous other quieter revolutions were going on: against a hierarchical traditionalism based on heredity, against status-conscious formality in dress, against a perpetuation of history that ignored 99 percent of the people and whitewashed and idolized a few tyrants and generals.

Many people welcomed the collapse of what they regarded as corrupt and tyrannical authority at the top of the nation's government in the forced resignation of the American President in the Watergate affair. It was the ultimate downfall of authority that many Americans greeted with jubilation.

The open protest against all authority is abundantly apparent in Terkel's collection of workers' interviews. The boss is no longer the venerated and feared father figure. Social divisions, exclusions, and one's own lowly social status are no longer philosophically accepted without question. Gone is the attitude that one's duty is to labor acquiescently in the system, thanking men like Ford and Rockefeller for saving America and providing one with a job. The owner is not inevitably right, and the American way of doing business is not automatically fair. The police officer is not always honest. The doctor is not always humane.

These anti-authoritarian positions, which had always been identified with the radical left and punished as treason in the 1950s, were, by the time of Terkel's interviews, held by workers in the mainstream.

THE ISSUES

As Studs Terkel writes in his introduction to *Working*, the interviews speak of the "violence" done by work to the spirit as well as to the body. Indeed, the usual topics one finds in labor fiction—of low wages, their practical effect on families, and union organizing—are raised comparatively infrequently in these interviews. The psychological damage, the injury done to the spirit, overwhelms the physical details.

Yet some physical details do emerge, not so much about wages, as about hours. A farmworker tells of his childhood when he would work from four A.M. to six A.M., before school, and from four P.M. until seven P.M. after school; a miner remembering working from six A.M. until ten P.M. in the 1930s; a hotel switchboard operator reports working 125 hours in a two-week time period without overtime pay; a salesman and payment collector works 72 hours a week; an interstate trucker works a 16-hour day. Each of these people speaks of the harm these work hours inflict on their family life and their own personal development. They have no time to just invite their souls. Some continue to work in their dreams.

Many encounter hazards on the job. The perils for paper deliverers, mail carriers, and meter readers are vicious dogs that have been known to rip at a worker's throat and face. Illnesses among farmworkers are substantially higher than the average for industry as a whole. They are subject to severe back problems from stoop labor, pesticide poisoning, and heatstroke. Coal miners report on-the-job deaths of many friends when mines collapse or heavy equipment hits them. Large numbers of them end up suffering from black lung disease caused by coal dust. Garbage collectors are hit by metal, heavy lumber, flying glass, and even acid as garbage is compacted on the truck. Janitors, who must carry heavy loads of trash down stairs and shovel huge quantities of snow in winter, are typically plagued by heart attacks.

Factory workers face multiple occupational risks. A spot welder is burned continually on the face and arms by flying sparks. His clothes catch on fire, and he is also subject to cuts, blood poisoning, and falling and flying metal. "I got hit square in the chest one day with a bar from a rock and it cut me down the side. They didn't take x-rays or nothing. Sent me back on the job" (224). Another spot welder describes one night when a worker on an assembly line fell to his knees, bleeding profusely after being hit in the head with a welding gun. The most important thing to the foreman, who did not call an ambulance even though the man required five stitches in his head, was to rush over the prostrate man to turn the assembly line back on after it had been turned off. A woman working in a luggage factory explains that workers constantly carry scars from burns. One of her fellow workers had a hand injured by severe burns and lost two fingers when a large piece of rusty equipment broke and fell on her. Her workplace often reaches 150 degrees. Police officers face being wounded or killed even when walking a beat, and firefighters must live with hazards daily in burning, collapsing buildings.

Wages are low, hours are long, hopes for advancement are thwarted, unions are too often less than helpful, and workplace accidents and health hazards are unrelenting realities. But the workers interviewed by Studs Terkel more often concentrate, not on these ever-present details, but on larger issues. They take into consideration the whole economic system of owners and workers. They touch on moral issues at work perpetuated by that system. Most of all, they examine what their work has done to their spirits, their sense of selfhood, their place as individual human beings: the way in which the system constantly dehumanizes them by trying to turn them into machines; the humiliations they suffer; the utter lack of appreciation on the part of the public, the customers they serve, and their bosses; and their feelings of having never made marks in the world with what they do and never being able to have pride in what they do—for example, never even seeing the finished product in which their work is invested.

THE SYSTEM

The basic system these workers see is one in which a few own all the wealth and the many work—first, to furnish the few with the wealth they enjoy and, second, to survive themselves. A freight elevator operator declares that those with wealth and power enjoy the things that the poor produce. He sees that the boss is concerned about their workers only "as it affects his production, where his profits are involved" (737). He looks forward to the day when a different system will take over and profits will be socialized. The president of a local union for automobile workers explains the system by saying that large industries put property value and profits before human beings. And a process clerk concludes that in this time of the Vietnam War, the system tells the poor that their sons are required to die for their country, but they are not really dying for their country; they are dying for a system that keeps a few people in power and wealth.

A farmworker remembers his daydreams in the field when he was a boy: "If I were a millionaire, I would buy all these ranches and give them back to the people" (33). As an adult, he comes to realize the illogical inhumanity of the system:

> I began to see how everything was so wrong. When growers can have an intricate watering system to irrigate their crops but they can't have running water inside the houses of workers. Veterinarians tend to the needs of domestic animals but they can't have medical care for the workers. They can have land subsidies for the growers but they can't have adequate unemployment compensation for the workers. ... They have heat and insulated barns for the animals but the workers live in beat-up shacks with no heat at all. (36)

A steelworker draws attention to a situation within the system in which the bosses make big money and the workers make barely enough to live on. He reads in the papers that fancy politicians give themselves thousand-dollar raises but protest when a steelworker asks for $.50 more an hour.

The system perpetuates a class division between those who work with their hands and those who do not, according to another steelworker, whose story serves as part of the preface. He introduces the reader to the sharp psychological divide between the common laborer and the person with a college education. Each resents the other and is defensive about his or her own position and work. The steelworker would like to run a bookstore and tavern where college students and workers could come together to talk.

One salesman, while he disapproves of some of the dishonest practices he knows about, declares that he is a capitalist and thinks that capitalism is the greatest system there is. But another ex-salesman has become disillusioned with commercialism, in which making money is the supreme value. His father, he says, believed in the American Dream of making money, even though he lost every penny he ever made. The son questions this. If someone sells merchandise for three times what it is worth, is that the American Dream? To be a salesperson is to be a con artist, he concludes. And to be a successful salesperson would involve constant "apple polishing." He could, he thinks, buy stock and be part of the system, but "I really question the system" (343). A car salesman concludes that if people and customers are rats, it is "the whole system that makes 'em animals" (309).

MORAL ISSUES AT WORK

Many workers question the morality of their companies' practices and the morality of the work they themselves are required to do. A poor Appalachian miner relates the story of his grandfather who, like other ordinary residents of the area, sold the mineral rights of the land he owned to get enough money to live on. Now the area is one of the richest in natural resources in the world, and its people are among the poorest. The resources are all owned by huge companies. To harvest these resources— gas, oil, coal—the companies tear the top of the ground away and pollute the streams with oil and chemicals. The miner reports that his son, a Vietnam veteran, claimed that he came back to his home county in the United States to find it more of a wasteland than battle areas napalmed in Vietnam.

Ad writers and salespeople are morally troubled by the shoddy products they push. One writer/producer calls herself a hustler who is troubled by the lies she writes to sell cosmetics to women who want but never get a timeless face. She continues even though she is convinced that what she does is neither necessary nor does she perform a service. Rip Torn, an actor, sees actors as the tools of businesspeople and politicians, pretending to be artistic conveyors of truth and beauty. A telephone solicitor despises her job and is ashamed of it because the most successful solicitor is the best liar. Because of this, she often leaves her post after a phone call to throw up, and she ends her work day weeping.

It is a system run on commercialism. A man who makes his living selling merchandise out of a catalog door to door and then collecting payments from those who buy on time appears to be ambiguous about a system fueled by commercial values and greed. He deplores his time as a bait and switch furniture salesman who would close a sale by showing the customer "the bait"—a nice piece of furniture—and then switch and deliver a shoddy piece of furniture. Most merchandise in the United States is sold by the bait and switch method, he declares. But he resents his daughter-in-law telling him that he exploits people.

A police officer, generally satisfied with his job, still is ashamed of the fact that the real criminals in his city—those who control vice and gambling—are never arrested. A photographer observes that most of her fellow photographers have little scruples about making photographs that she would refuse to make—of embarrassing situations and violence. In the last case, she believes the photographer should be stepping in to stop the violence, not photographing it.

Factory workers report that, on the assembly line, faulty parts are allowed to proceed. Part of this is a kind of sabotage on the part of the worker. Part of it results from the owners' refusal to maintain inspections that would require expensive rebuilding. Those workers who persist in calling attention to flaws are labeled troublemakers. In these cases, it is not so much the status of their work, but the immorality of what it involves that causes them to have little pride in what they do.

THE PUBLIC'S VIEW OF THE JOB

Working men and women are perfectly aware of the status of their work in society and among their family and friends. Sometimes the low repute of their work grates on them. In some cases, they are able to keep the nature of their work concealed from friends and relatives. Unexpectedly, in several cases, workers claim that they are satisfied with what they do, in spite of the public denigration of their work. For some, it boils down to the public's lack of appreciation for what workers spend their lives doing.

Women, relegated to lower status jobs, are belittled by bosses and owners who are inevitably male. A young college graduate with a major in English has difficulty finding a job after graduation and must settle for a job as a receptionist. At parties she will enjoy being engaged in intelligent conversation with other guests. But when they learn that she is a receptionist, she gets an odd, almost disapproving look, and they walk away. Just the label convinces others that she is not worth bothering with. A hotel switchboard operator suffers under the same burden of disrespect from bosses, guests, and the general public. One aspect of this is the mode of address. Managers, assistant managers, and buyers, all male, are called "mister," but the operators, all female, are addressed by their first names. A bank teller complains that she is snubbed at parties when she reveals what she does for a living, and that again, whereas all the men who sit at desks in the bank are referred to as "mister," the tellers, usually female, are addressed by their first names. The flight attendant's little sisters and her working-class neighbors hold her in awe because of her job, but in the big city, she reports, "flight attendant" is synonymous with loose woman, and the other women they meet are cold and suspicious of them. A waitress is frequently asked, by people who are impressed by her, why she is "just" a waitress. It is not her job that she does not like, it is the denigration that she endures that makes her resentful.

The hurt that workers in other service areas feel from lack of prestige is intense. They feel abused by their clientele, who regard them as servants. The collector of payments for merchandise bought on time confesses that his grown children find what he does to be demeaning and exploitative, a view that he is finally forced to share. Day after day, 'every time he knocks on a door and senses someone inside has recognized him, he is greeted with, "'Aw, [s—]!'" (135) "Can you imagine what happens to you, hearing this all day long?" (135) A car salesman bitterly observes that he is always ridiculed in social situations as one who cannot be trusted because of his job.

An ex-salesman who has taken a job as a janitor after having a nervous breakdown feels that his new job is a blow to his ego and lies to his friends about what he does. A barber complains that the public regards him as a nobody and that he avoids telling people outside the shop what his trade is. A hairstylist feels abused by his customers who regard him as a servant.

The steelworker who opens the preface says that what bothers him is the failure of other people to recognize the worth of what he does. To label a woman "just" a housewife or a worker "just" a laborer is demeaning. A truck driver who hauls steel complains that among the people with whom he associates in a status-conscious environment, truck driving is the lowliest job. He believes that everyone has some respect from management except the driver. Even outside the steel mill he hauls for, he suffers a low status. For example, state troopers, he says, look on truckers as outlaws and thieves. And it never occurs to the companies they work for or the Teamsters union they represent to stand up for truckers against troopers who harass them. A woman who works in a factory explains how she was even belittled by others at a conference of the Governor's Commission on the Status of Women. "You felt like a little piece of scum ... just because we worked in a factory" (389).

Farmworkers and garbage collectors report being taunted on the job and called insulting names. Townspeople observing farmworkers, driving into town with family members crowded into trucks, laugh and point at them, shouting, "Here comes the carnival!" (33).

DEHUMANIZATION

Probably the most pervasive complaint of both white- and blue-collar workers in Terkel's interviews is that their jobs, as they are regarded by the system, dehumanize them. They are not regarded as individuals and so feel that their humanity is taken from them. Over and over again, workers complain that they are not recognized by owners and bosses as persons; this is stated by people who do vastly different jobs: a farmworker—"[T]he growers don't recognize us as persons" (38); an airline flight attendant—"They call us professional people but they talk to us as very young childishly" (80); a professor of surgery—"A hospital is a dehumanizing institution" (642); a patient's representative—"I don't have any identification marks as a person" (646); and a steelworker—"You're not regarded. You're just a number out there" (716).

The mechanization of the Industrial Revolution, which occurred in the eighteenth century, never becomes less alarming or more acceptable to the worker, 200 years later. A surprising number of workers express shock and outrage at being looked upon as machines, subjugated by machines, or being integral parts of a larger machine. The machine, as a figure of speech, often used by the sociologist and historian, naturally seeps into the discourse of the workers themselves, both educated and uneducated. A balanced view of the machine is provided by a steelworker, who believes that the machine, including the computer, can work for the good or ill of the worker. If it takes away all the work of human beings, takes away their livelihoods entirely, then it is an agent of destruction, but if it is used to make humans' work less arduous, it can be an instrument for good. It is not the machine that is inherently bad, he observes, but the way in which mankind puts it to use.

Many workers feel an injustice regarding machines and tools: that is, that machines and implements are more valued than workers and are treated better than workers. A heavy equipment operator notes that the owners value their machines, costing more than a quarter of a million dollars, much more than they do their human workers, who receive low wages. He asks why the worker is not worth as much money as a machine. The assembly line worker also says that the machine gets better care, more attention, and greater respect than the workers.

Workers have the feeling that they are enslaved to machines. The receptionist who must answer phones constantly says the machine, in the form of the telephone, controls her life. All day long when it rings, she is compelled to answer it. She names her idea of heaven "no-phone." Even a stockbroker says he is struggling against the machine, his word for the system itself.

A farmworker observes that the laborers are not regarded as human beings but as farm implements. A telephone operator declares that she is just an instrument. A former airlines reservationist says that she had no free will: "I was just part of that stupid computer" (83). A receptionist declares that her job does not mean anything because, not only is she dictated to by a machine, but she is nothing more than a little machine herself. A bank teller is resigned to the fact that her bosses want the tellers to be machines, to dehumanize employees: "It's like I'm almost being treated as a machine" (350). Even the cabdrivers feel dehumanized. One of them says that nobody cares about them. They are, he declares, machines, just like the run-down cabs they drive. So does a truck driver, who says the only way he can get through the tense days of driving a truck and being humiliated by bosses, merchants, and troopers is to regard himself as a machine.

Those who are most plagued by the machine are those who work on assembly lines, for the machine dictates how fast they themselves must work. The spot welder in a Ford assembly plant must move constantly as the machine brings a part of the automobile to him and takes it away, not at the welder's pace but at the "line's" pace. He says the only time the workers stop moving is when the line stops moving. If you fall behind in your work, you bump into the next worker on the line which starts a chain reaction all the way down the line. The foremen rarely turn off the assembly line, even for injured workers. The plant urges the foremen to use stopwatches to increase efficiency. One worker turned union man says such moves are mechanical, not human.

The spot welder reveals that he is nothing more than a machine. A stock chaser working on the assembly line for Ford Motor Company confesses that he felt like he was a robot. The president of a local union who worked on the assembly line explains how the lines are studied and arranged to make things more efficient and productive—"like a robot," he says. A steelworker asserts that he is "not like a machine. Well, a machine wears out too sometimes" (715).

ASPIRING TO SOMETHING HIGHER

One of the most discouraging aspects of being unhappy in one's work is being unable to reach a higher plane on one's job—a promotion that says, "You are appreciated." A police officer wants desperately to be a detective. He thinks he has qualities of leadership, but those higher up do not respect him—except as cannon fodder. A spot welder, who must stand all day in one spot and do the same job over and over, would like to be a utility man who can move about the plant and perform a variety of jobs.

But even more melancholy is the person who is never able to reach the vocation they think is right for them. A woman who cleans other people's houses confesses that what she has wanted to do all her life is to play the piano, write songs, and record stories about her childhood. At least one laborer, who says work on an assembly line at Ford is worse than being in jail, has genuine hope of escaping after graduating from college.

MAKING A MARK

Many attest to the fact that the most spiritually hurtful aspect of their jobs is the realization that they have nothing to point to as an accomplishment. They never make a mark. A steelworker observes that a laborer like himself cannot point with pride to a house he has constructed, like the builder of old. He sums up the problem:

> I would like to see a building, say, the Empire State, I would like to see on one side of it a foot-wide strip from top to bottom with the name of every bricklayer, the name of every electrician, with all the names. So when a guy walked by, he could take his son and say, "See, that's me over there on the forty-fifty floor. I put the steel beam in." ... Everybody should have something to point to. (2)

The man who works on an assembly line never sees the final product. A steelworker confides that he sometimes puts a tiny dent in the piece of the steel he is working on, just so he can believe he has made his mark: "I'd like to make my imprint" (10).

This desire to make a mark is as strong among office workers as it is among those who do hard labor with their hands. A receptionist operating a switchboard yearns to be building something like a piece of furniture, to fix something to make it work.

Sometimes the desire to make a mark with one's work is another way of saying that one wishes one's work had meaning. A government administrator states the problem in a different way; he wishes that his work had a positive impact on other people: "I don't see this work as meaning anything" (450).

LIKING AND HATING ONE'S WORK

Most of the people Studs Terkel interviewed despised what they had to do for a living: the steelworkers, the miners, the farmworkers, the receptionists and switchboard operators, those who worked for airlines, the telephone solicitor, the washroom attendants and janitors, the cleaning woman, the assembly line worker, the bus driver, the trucker, the hospital aide, and others. They hate the work because it is backbreaking, meaningless, a dead end, and a constant barrage of humiliations.

But several people Terkel interviewed liked their work a great deal. One of the most remarkable is the stonemason, one of the interviewees who opens the volume. The stonemason feels deeply that he has found his vocation, the work he was born to do. Furthermore, he is proud of the long tradition of the mason, going back to the Egyptian pyramids. Stone, he says, is his life. His work allows him to be an artist, a mathematician, an engineer, a naturalist. When he is not actually performing his work, he is daydreaming about it. He knows the location of every piece of work he has ever created, whether it be a garden wall or a fireplace, and if he wants, he can revisit it. His work is his immortality. A worker with equal passion for his job is a piano tuner. He knows that his work is an art and that he has thoroughly mastered it. He enjoys it and uses it to enlarge his mastery of music.

A construction worker sees his immortality in his work: the road he had worked on, the medical building he worked on, the bridge he helped build. He has pride in these things and can say, "I did that" (54). One police officer, though he has serious complaints on the job, calls it "one of the most gratifying jobs in the world." Another thinks he is there to help people. Citizens look up to him. He remembers saving the life of a child. A firefighter says that you can actually see a firefighter produce.

A housewife feels guilty because she loves her work so much. A pharmacist who loves working gets the appreciation of his clientele, one of whom tells him he does great things for humanity. A real estate saleswoman, somewhat her own boss, loves her job because she has interaction with people and believes she is helping them.

A labor organizer boasts: "I'm one of the few people I know who was lucky in life to find out what he really wanted to do. I'm just havin' a ball, the time of my life" (467). He thinks he is not only helping workers with specific problems, he believes he is improving a bad system. A librarian says she would never retire because she loves her work so much. She is her own boss, initiates things, experiments, and works to get children interested in reading.

It does not take much to see what makes one person hate his or her work and other workers love theirs. It is not the danger of the work or how hard it is physically. It has much to do with one's freedom on the job, with feeling like he or she is working up to his or her potential, of being able to make a positive difference in the lives of others and of being appreciated. Happy workers see their work as giving them meaning and immortality.

QUESTIONS AND PROJECTS

As a class, create a volume of interviews for the twenty-first century, modeled on Terkel's record for the twentieth century.

1. Write brief rationales for your suggestions about basic questions most interviewees should be asked. Then through class discussion, agree on a list, adding and eliminating submitted questions as the group sees fit.
2. As a class, agree on the workers to be interviewed. Make a case for each choice, including those whose jobs are especially pertinent to your geographic area and to the twenty-first century.
3. Do research for two or three class periods on the most productive way to conduct interviews and print the guideline agreed upon. For example, how will you approach your interviewee and explain what you would like to do? Where will your interview be conducted? What will you wear? How will you unobtrusively set up audio tape recording? How will you begin the conversation? Will you ever interrupt your interviewee? How will you make him or her at ease and forthcoming?
4. Do careful and thorough research on the history and background of the work in which your interviewee is involved. When did that particular vocation begin and where? How has it changed over the years? If big companies are involved, what are the major ones?

Has the trade or the company been in the news in the last several years? Is the interviewee's job unionized? What has been the history of attempts to unionize and, if applicable, the history of the union's work and issues? Write an essay on your findings.

5. Arrange, plan, and design the volume the class has created for binding. Deposit one copy in your school library and one in each of the nearest public libraries. Another more ambitious project would be to plan an advertising project for your book using the Web and other resources, and print and bind copies on demand.

FURTHER READING

Abruzzi, Adam. *Workers and Work Measurement*. New York: Columbia University Press, 1956.

Applesbaum. Herbert. *Work in Market and Industrial Society*. Albany, NY: State University of New York Press, 1984.

Bell, Daniel. *Work and Its Discontents: The Cult of Efficiency in America*. Boston: Beacon Press, 1956.

Cleeton, Glen. U. *Making Work Human*. Antioch, OH: Antioch Press, 1949.

Feldman, Richard and Michael Betzold, eds. *End of the Line: Autoworkers of the American Dream*. New York: Weidenfeld and Nicolson, 1988.

Goldberg, Roberta. *Organizing Women Office Workers*. New York: Praeger Publishers, 1983.

Gutman, Herbert G. *Work, Culture, and Society in Industrializing America*. New York: Vintage, 1977.

Halle, David. *America's Working Man*. Chicago: University of Chicago Press, 1984.

Heron, Alexander Richard. *Why Men Work*. New York: Arno Press, 1977.

Santoro, Victor. *Fighting Back on the Job*. Port Townsend, WA: Loompanics Unlimited, 1984.

Sheppard, Harold L. and Neal Q. Herrick. *Where Have All of the Robots Gone? Worker Dissatisfaction in the Seventies*. New York: The Free Press, 1972.

Terkel, Studs. *Working*. New York: Ballantine Books, 1972.

Widick, B.J., ed. *Auto Work and Its Discontents*. Baltimore, MD: The Johns Hopkins University Press, 1976.

9

Zilpha Snyder's *The Velvet Room,* Joan Bauer's *Hope Was Here,* and Anne Mazer's *Working Days*

In the twentieth and twenty-first centuries, authors of fiction for young adults have sometimes turned their attention to children who work. In the late 1960s and early 1970s, the pattern of child labor was transformed chiefly by the growth of the fast-food industry as well as the independence children experienced in the 1960s. Zilpha Snyder's *The Velvet Room,* a highly popular, prize-winning novel that appeared in 1965, was part of that new dynamic, even though it is set in the 1930s. Two other books on children working were published at the turn of the twenty-first century: Anne Mazer's collection of short fiction on adolescent work titled *Working Days: Short Stories About Teenagers at Work* (1997) and Joan Bauer's *Hope Was Here* (2002) the story of a teenage waitress. These three works—as well as other popular young adult fiction set in the late twentieth and early twenty-first centuries—do bring the reader into the mind of the working child and show the importance and meaning of the work experience; however, they tend to paint a rosier picture of child and adolescent labor than the facts bear out.

THE HISTORY OF CHILD LABOR

The history of child labor is overwhelmingly a long and sordid story. Even before the Industrial Revolution, poor children had been put to work as soon as they could walk. One has only to be reminded of conditions, even before the Industrial Revolution, when toddlers worked in the agricultural fields and children as young as four years had the full care of infants. That history includes tiny children being put to work as chimney sweeps and children working on the streets of cities selling matches and newspapers as they did well into the twentieth century in England and the United States. It includes children whose bodies were sold by their parents, and homeless children who were put to work as pickpockets by criminals.

After the Industrial Revolution poor children were forced to work under the most treacherous of conditions. For example, in mines, where children were hired in part because they were small and could crawl into small spaces, they routinely died as tunnels collapsed, materials exploded, and heavy carts crashed along underground. In factories they became mangled in hazardous machinery.

Ironically, the modest improvements in medicine and sanitation in the eighteenth century increased the birth rate and therefore the numbers of children,; providing industrialists with more fodder for their factories. Factory owners were eager to take advantage of a potentially large work-force that was obedient, easy to control, and could be had for cheap wages. As workers, children were imminently more desirable than the hostile adult laborers who were, at the same time, encouraging the growth of unions to respond to untenable working conditions. These circumstances, after the Industrial Revolution, led to a far more cruel and inhumane exploitation and abuse of children than had been seen before.

In colonial America, children began working, without pay, in home industries doing laundry and making parts of shoes, hats, and dresses. This practice continued without regulation for more than 300 years—until the Fair Labor Standards Act of 1938. Colonial Americans considered children over the age of six years to be adults, so they were typically apprenticed to tradesmen at that age. In U.S. cities in the nineteenth and early twentieth centuries, children of immigrants were put to work in sweatshops to help the family meet basic living expenses.

Children were not a small, inconsequential portion of the factory workforce. Half of the textile mill workers in mid-nineteenth-century England and the United States were under the age of 20 years. (The rest were women workers.) Owners put children as young as 4 years old to work in textile mills and mines for 12 hours a day. Six-year-olds consti-tuted a significant portion of textile workers. The duties in both mills and mines were backbreaking and carried out at top speed. When children reached adulthood, they were fired so that less expensive workers could replace them. And the dismissed adult workers were forced out in the world without experience in or knowledge of any other work except that from which they were now barred.

Throughout periods of wholesale exploitation of child labor in England, humanitarians struggled against overwhelming odds for legislation to better the lives of children. After a decades-long campaign, for example, to help children forced into the dangerous work of chimney sweeps, a 1788 act was passed, regulating their work in England. In the 1830s, a reformer named Richard Oastler was able to establish what were known as Short Time Committees to limit the working hours of children to 10 per day. In 1833, one of the Factory Acts forbade textile workers to hire children under the age of nine years and to restrict the hours of child laborers to 13. Another Factory Act in 1842 forbade the hiring of small children in mines. Not until 1847 did the government limit the factory workday for children to 10 hours. But many jobs for children were unchanged by the Factory Act. One such exception was addressed when the Workshop Act forbade hiring children in large workshops.

In the United States, laws to regulate child labor were long in coming. With the spiraling, unregulated industrialization after the Civil War, two million children in the United States worked in harsh, dangerous circumstances for pittances. In the early twentieth century, compulsory schooling, as well as laws enacted by 28 states restricting child labor, decreased the numbers of working children, but two million children were still in the workforce, laboring 12 hours a day, six days a week. For the children who remained in the workforce, state legislation in the early twentieth century had little reliable protection. These laws were ambiguous, full of loopholes, and poorly enforced. In 1904, the National Child Labor Committees worked to reform child labor, and further restrictive laws were passed from 1904 to 1909. When in 1916 President Woodrow Wilson urged a law protecting children called the Keating-Owen Child Labor Act, it was overturned in 1918, two years later, by the Supreme Court. In the same year, Congress, determined to regulate child labor, passed a second law, similar to Keating-Owen, and it, too, was overturned by the Supreme Court. In 1924, Congress offered a constitutional amendment to protect child workers. It was vigorously fought by big and small businesses, so it was scarcely surprising that it failed to pass a referendum by eight states. Not until 1938 was effective federal legislation passed to protect child laborers, and even this had many loopholes. For example, it did not extend to children who labored in the fields. A law passed in 1950 did a better job of regulating child labor.

THE VELVET ROOM

One of the most popular young adult novels of recent years is Zilpha Snyder's *The Velvet Room,* about agricultural work and migrancy in the pursuit of work in the 1930s and its effect on the family. The plot, as seen from the view of Robin, a 12-year-old girl, centers on a family of migrants, well-educated people, who have been forced into unemployment and have for two years traveled constantly from place to place so that the frail father can look for work. As the story opens, the family's wreck of a car has broken down and Robin's father and older brother have gone in search of help to get the car repaired and get on the road again. Fortuitously, in a trek to find help with the car, they also find what they have been in search of for two years—a job that comes with living quarters.

Robin, an adventurer, has several meaningful encounters in their new home. First, in her wanderings, she becomes friends with a mysterious old woman, a hermit considered by the children in the area to be a witch. With the old woman's help, she is able to explore an abandoned mansion in which she finds a "velvet room," basically an ornate library. Her other encounter is with the daughter of the man who owns the agricultural business for which her father works. In their more comfortable pre-Great Depression lives, Robin has been well educated in literature and music and is a superb pianist. She is warmly admitted into the owner's household, where she tutors her new friend in music and other studies.

But no sooner has the family settled in than circumstances develop to threaten them with another dreaded move. Their father is in a physical decline and is no longer able to perform the backbreaking work he faces each day in the fields. Their only option seems to be moving to the home of their stingy, disagreeable uncle who needs someone to tend his store. Robin, however, is offered a way out. The owner's family invites her to remain with them, where she can live in comfort in a beautiful house in exchange for her skills at tutoring and encouraging their daughter. But after making up her mind to remain behind, she reverses herself at the last minute, refusing their offer in order to stay with her family. By this time, the historical commission of the area, led by the owner, has made arrangements to turn the mansion and the velvet room into an historical site.

Shortly before Robin's family is to leave, she visits the velvet room for one last time. There she encounters young thieves, whom she recognizes, trying to loot the mansion of its treasures. In the process of valiantly struggling with the thieves to protect the velvet room, she is seriously injured.

In the end, her father is offered the job of custodian and guard of the mansion, which will be restored and open to the public. And the family will be provided with a charming cottage to live in.

The Issues in *The Velvet Room*

The Velvet Room is primarily about the effect on the children of the father's employment and unemployment. The perpetual moving from one short-term job to another, living in the car and a tent, has profoundly affected Robin, perhaps because the vagrant life of poverty is in such contrast to the life the family lived before their father lost his job in the Great Depression. The children must adjust to a new school several times a year. One result is Robin's frequent removal from reality: "Everything seemed to be moving backward away from her, getting smaller and smaller, less and less real" (5). She and her older brother and sister are especially disturbed by the precariousness of their existence, as when, for example, their old car breaks down and when they must face another move to their uncle's house. But, for Robin, even if they have to move, the velvet room will linger on as one of the few constants in her life.

Robin and her older sister are also deeply affected by the ridicule of native Californians. They remember continually and painfully an instance when in their jalopy piled high with their belongings, the townspeople pointed and laughed at them as they drove through town.

Another issue raised is the depressing impact on the family of their shoddy living quarters. Although they are pleased to be living in a shack instead of a tent or the car, they are discouraged by the housing provided by the owner. What looks to be a temporary shack sits up on posts and has not been painted in years. Most of all, Robin and the other children are terrified by the devastating physical impact on their father of the arduous work he must perform.

The Context

Despite Snyder's recognition of some of the problems of the children of migrant farm workers, a comparison of *The Velvet Room* with John Steinbeck's *Grapes of Wrath* and the actual historical context reveals how the author has elided over and softened the harsh realities suffered by the large majority of families in California during the Great Depression.

For example, most migrant farm workers in the 1930s were dirt poor and uneducated, even before they had been forced into a life of migrancy.

And, unlike those in *The Velvet Room*, children of migrants had no choice but to enter the fields as workers themselves, even at very young ages, because the adults could not harvest sufficient amounts of fruits and vegetables alone to earn a livable wage.

Moreover, Robin's friendship with the owner's family stretches the imagination. Even though Robin allays the mother's initial suspicions of her with her skill as a pianist, in reality, the sharp divide between owners and, especially, migrant workers, makes such a happy relationship highly unlikely.

HOPE WAS HERE

A second novel, dealing more directly with work, is Joan Bauer's award-winning *Hope Was Here*, a portrait of the life of a 16-year-old member of the workforce. It is an enlightening account of the skills that a young waitress brings to her job. It is the view, however, of an energetic young person, not that of a seasoned employee who has been on her feet carrying heavy trays for a span of 20 or 30 years. Nor does Hope, the main character, seem to grasp how grueling waiting tables can be for the career waitress. Still, it is a positive picture of adolescent work.

The Plot

Hope Was Here is told in first person by Hope, a 16-year-old who has been waiting on tables in a variety of restaurants since she was 14 years old. She is troubled by having been deserted by her mother, also a waitress, when she was a sickly newborn still in the hospital. Hope and her loving and supportive Aunt Addie, who adopted her, live the lives of migrants, moving from town to town, following Addie's promise of work as a cook. Hope's story opens with still another move, this time from Brooklyn to a diner in Mulhoney, Wisconsin. Her story will end in this novel with another transition—from the Mulhoney high school to Michigan State University.

Hope fills the reader in on her background: her desertion by her mother, the hope she has that someday her father will find her, the ridiculous name (Tulip) given her by her mother, her decision to change her name to Hope, and her mother's lack of interest in her, having shown up for a few hours only three times in Hope's life.

Her first act of independence and self-definition takes place when she changes her name from the hated Tulip to Hope. It not only demonstrates her choice, it describes an integral part of who she is, represents what life brings to her and how she wishes to regard the future.

At the story's opening, her favorite of the many places they have lived in is the location they must leave—the Blue Box Café in Brooklyn. Addie had co-owned the café with a man named Gleason Beal, who has disappeared with the money from their joint bank account. This subsequently forces them to close the restaurant.

To survive, Addie has found a job as manager and cook in a diner whose owner is suffering from leukemia. One of the attractions is that they will be furnished with an apartment on the premises.

The core of Hope's story is her experience in their new location at the diner, Welcome Stairways, in Mulhoney, Wisconsin. Here, through their work, she and Addie are bound to an array of characters. Chief among them is G. T. Stoop, a brave, kind diner owner who challenges corrupt local government, marries Addie, adopts Hope, and dies of leukemia. His employees include Flo, a wise and capable waitress; Yuri, a Russian émigré who works as a busboy; Lou Ellen, a waitress who initially regards Hope as a threat; and Braverman, also a high school student and an apprentice cook with whom Hope fall in love. The corrupt politicians challenged by Stoop are Mayor Eli Millstone and Sheriff L. Greebs. In addition to his employees, Stoop's supporters are an African American assistant sheriff named Brenda Babcock, a minister named Al B Hall, and an army of young people led by high schooler Adam Pulver.

The major action of the novel is Stoop's decision to run for mayor against the corrupt Mayor Millstone. Stoop uncovers a crooked operation in the mammoth Real Fresh Dairy that dictates to the town, exposing that the dairy has escaped paying local taxes for five years. The tax assessor's office had closed its doors for fear of public discovery of its own duplicity in the crimes.

The struggle proceeds with dirty campaigning. A hearse is parked in front of the diner to remind voters that D. L. has leukemia. A mouse is planted in a salad by a couple paid by Millstone. Braverman is brutally beaten. And the roll of voters includes townspeople who have never registered. Subplots include Hope's continual dream of finding her father, her confrontation of her mother, her daily attempt to come to terms with having been deserted, and her need for a father. On a happier note, she discovers that Braverman, the young man she admires, is also in love with her, and she is delighted with the courtship and marriage of Addie and D. L.

The Food Business

Waitressing is at the center of Hope's world and the story she narrates. The diner itself is the main setting of the novel where most of the action takes place. The reader sees Hope at work here—not attending the high school, which takes up most of her day. She and Addie actually live in the diner, as does the novel's hero, G. T. Stoop. Campaign events take place primarily in the diner: round table discussions of strategy, the investigating and writing of news stories, and even the dirty tricks played by the mayor. G. T. proposed to Addie in the diner, and the wedding reception food is prepared there. Hope and Bravermen's first date is there. G. T. dies in their apartment above the diner, and his wake is held in the diner.

Hope's absent mother is a career waitress whose only contribution to Hope's life is an occasional letter with suggestions about doing one's job well. She writes to Hope about the need for a good waitress to "keep the coffee coming and add up the check in her head" (29). On Hope's thirteenth birthday, while she was still busing tables, her mother visited, leaving her the three main rules for a waitress to follow: for a waitress, the cook is always right, the customer is always right, and if you can't arbitrate a disagreement between the two, you can forget a tip. Hope's mother also has some wisdom regarding customers. Cheap tippers were probably unhappy as children; eating low-fat meals leaves customers unsatisfied; men tip better when not accompanied by their girlfriends; and parents love waitresses who are friendly with their children. She also advises Hope to talk to the regular customers, remember what they say, and continue the conversations when the customers return (43).

At another time, her mother gives her more subtle hints: put lemon wedges under the counter so that they can be produced instantly; keep painkillers in your pocket for customers; and tell customers what salad dressings are available rather than just asking them what they want (143).

Hope observes many things about food service on her own and she takes pride in the skills and knowledge she brings to her job. Upon arriving in Wisconsin to work in a new diner, she knows that mastering the menu is the best preparation she can bring to the job. She is confident in her new job because she has had experience in working both counters and tables, can carry five platters on one arm, and can speedily, correctly, and calmly wait on a number of tables at one time when the diner is "deep in the weeds," or overwhelmed with customers (36).

The chief demands and satisfactions of the job are psychological rather than physical. She takes pleasure in enticing customers to try new foods, in surprising the grill man by apologizing even though he had made the mistake, in knowing how to "connect with people" (47). Hope has a positive philosophical outlook on the meaning of her work:

> [W]hen you're in food service, you understand that sometimes you're making up for people in your customers' lives who haven't been too nice. A lonely old woman at the counter just lights up when I smile at her, a tired mother with a screaming baby squeezes my hand when I clean up the mess her other child spilled.
>
> You know what I like most about waitressing? When I'm doing it, I'm not thinking that much about myself. I'm thinking about other people. I'm learning again and again what it takes to make a difference in people's lives. (144)

Hope's work makes up for much pain and loss in her life. Her regular customers and her coworkers substitute for an extended family. And her job gives her self-definition and independence, equal to choosing her own name. Her success in her job brings her self-assurance, self-worth, and pride.

Her mastery of her vocation also brings continuity to her transient life. Her residence, school, and friends are always changing, but waitressing remains a constant in her life, and her skills provide her with continuity.

Her job also brings her life meaning. She believes that she has made her mark with each job, an attitude that she symbolizes by leaving a literal mark in each diner she works in, writing "Hope Was Here" in some unobtrusive place. "Whenever I leave a place I write it real small someplace significant just to make the statement that I'd been there and made an impact" (3).

Despite her enthusiasm for her work, Hope's story raises several work issues relative to food service. Prominent among these is the instability of the restaurant business that forces Addie, a chef, to move from job to job. Addie seems resigned to the constant moving, but a migrant life takes a heavy toll on children like Hope. By the time they reach Wisconsin, Hope has moved nine times. No sooner does she make friends and begin to feel at home than the restaurant where Addie works closes down or she gets fired and they have to leave. Before one of the moves, when Hope was 10, she runs away from Addie and hides, eventually dragging herself back, afraid she will be abandoned again, to scream and attack the car, packed with their belongings. It is not only the problem of being forced to leave behind home, friends, school, and familiar surroundings;

it is having to learn to survive in a new location among new faces. Hope believes this adversity has made her tough. On her first day of school in Pensacola, Florida, when she was in the eighth grade, she stood in the middle of the basketball court and shouted, "'Look, does anyone here want to be my friend?'" (12)

One problem of the waitress opens the novel: that is great pressure on the job to deal calmly with difficult patrons and to move lots of food fast without dropping anything. Hope got her first waitressing job at the age of 14 years when one of her coworkers broke down in hysterics after spilling soup on a difficult customer and being yelled at by her boss for crying. The constant need for presenting a composed, cheerful demeanor is hard on servers who, like Lou Ellen, are experiencing disturbing personal problems. She also mentions (what many different kinds of workers complain of) being so busy that she cannot go to the bathroom. Yet Hope presents all these problems, not as if they are job issues, but as if they are weaknesses of character in the waitresses themselves. *She* is tough. *She* can handle things. And nothing in her story suggests any awakening to the contrary.

Problems of Waitpersons

Hope's work as a young adult is made less problematic and more enjoyable because she is not limited to a lifetime of waitressing. She has the opportunity at the end of her story to attend college. Still, Hope's mother and Flo, her coworker in Welcome Stairways, both representative of career waitressing in the novel, attest to a lifetime of satisfying work with few problems. Yet according to nonfictional accounts, the work presents waitresses, even the "tough" ones, with crucial difficulties.

Not only is there no time to use the bathroom, there is no time to eat and no time to sit down. Hope fails to mention how the low wages of most waitresses, kept low in part with the excuse that they will receive substantial tips, constitute real personal hardship. This is an area of work rarely represented by unions, which traditionally have bargained for higher wages and better conditions.

Waitresses complain of physical infirmities: the early arthritis and the back, foot, and leg pains that come from being constantly on one's feet for long hours. And emotional stress from dealing with unreasonable customers, coworkers, and managers, plus the obsession with pleasing the customers, contribute to a high instance of alcoholism among career waitresses.

Hope doesn't bring up another concern of young, vulnerable wait-resses: the sexual advances and innuendos of customers who assume that all waitresses have easy morals and will do anything for money. This atti-tude is consistent with the low status afforded waitresses generally.

WORKING DAYS

Edited by Anne Mazer, *Working Days* is a collection of short stories that covers a wide range of work done by young people. Some of these stories present a positive outlook on work. They show the joy of work, its capac-ity to give meaning and enlightenment to the lives of young workers, and, most of all, the rich associations that work offers them.

The Stories

Several of the main characters have specific aspirations, as professionals.

In Magdalena Gomez's "The Daydreamer," a 14-year-old daughter of Puerto Rican and Spanish parents, decides to ignore her parents' wishes by getting a job in a supermarket so that she can make enough money to go to Spain to learn to dance. But before she actually applies for the job, her school principal offers her a job as a Spanish tutor, and she modi-fies her ambition to leave for Spain at once. In Lois Metger's "Seashell Motel," a 16-year-old lies about her age and assumes a new name in order to get a job out of town in a fancy motel for the summer. Her job is an escape into another identity. In Carolina Hospital's "Catskill Snows," a young woman is thwarted in her aspiration to sing with the Cuban band her mother and stepfather manage because her mother wants a more respectable future for her. And the chief character of Nora Daudenhauer's "Egg Boat" is a young Eskimo girl who proudly learns the trade of fishing in her own little boat.

"The Crash Room" (meaning a hospital emergency room) by David Rice is about a doctor who looks back on his teenage years working in the emergency room of a hospital, visiting the morgue, and finally find-ing that the constant death of people he has come to know in the crash room has overcome him. He is able to become a doctor by focusing on childbirth and life.

At the heart of several work stories is the young person's encounter with an inspiring elderly person. The important idea in Roy Hoffman's "Ice Cream Man" is the young ice-cream vendor's encounter with an ancient black man with whom he chatted on the job and provided with free ice cream until, after a brief absence, he returns to find that his friend has died. Kim Stafford's "Riding Up to Ruby's" and Marilyn Sachs's "Lessons" have similar themes of the value of the associations they makes, especially with older people, in the course of one's job. In the former, a teenage boy takes a job caring for an elderly woman with whom he develops a deep bond. In the latter, a young girl named Charlotte gives English lessons to an elderly man, who becomes a father substitute.

Several of the stories raise workplace issues. In Victor Martinez's "The Baseball Glove," two brothers go to work picking fruit in the fields. Manny, who tells the story, is working to buy a new baseball glove. But the glove is purchased at great price, for after farmworkers pick at top speed throughout the morning, lugging heavy bags in the boiling heat, the immigration service raids the fields, scattering illegal workers, who are forced to leave behind many bags of produce they have picked. Manny, who is sickened by what he sees, is able to get the money for his glove by selling, with his brother, the produce picked at such great price by the fleeing men.

In "Delivery in a Week," by Thylias Moss, a young girl working as a telephone solicitor makes contact with a desperate woman whose daughter has disappeared from home, an encounter that gives her motivation to work for charity and social service organizations.

"The Pill Factory" by Anne Mazer is the story of a teenager, used to all manner of bottom-level work, who is used to hearing her father say, "Work or die." After taking a job in a pill factory, she meets two women hardened by years of demeaning work in which she now shares:

> Mechanically, I thrust label after label through the glue machine. My stiffened fingers worked in an automatic rhythm. I had a numbing feeling of unreality, as if I would never leave this factory, would never stop the endless round of bottles and labels. (92)

The monotony of being chained to the glue machine is worsened in the summer because of heat, the lack of air-conditioning, and the dirt rising from the floor and machines. The plight of a new employee—an older woman—enlists her sympathy.

"Forty Bucks" by Graham Salisbury highlights the danger of working in a fast-food restaurant at night. As with many of the stories in this collection, the two boys terrorized by thieves with a gun, stand in awe of an older customer (actually a police officer in street clothes) who manages to thwart the criminals.

Ann Hood's "The Avalon Ballroom" is the story of a single mother and her teenage daughter who live in a small, run-down apartment and struggle at poor paying jobs. Lily's job is at Baskin-Robbins. The urgency to find just a couple of thousand dollars more arises when she is accepted as a student at Princeton.

Tracy Marx's "To Walk with Kings" is about the custodial work required of two girls in a boarding school and their triumph over a new headmaster who is destroying the school with his management schemes of efficiency by turning all the girls into cleaners and cooks. And the main character, a teenager in Norman Wong's "Driver's License," finally realizes that life offers him more than the grind at McDonald's.

CHILD LABOR SINCE WORLD WAR II

Child labor subsided from the end of World War II until the 1980s. At that time, public concern over rising juvenile delinquency prompted President Reagan to appoint The President's Scientific Advisory Committee (1970) to rewrite laws to encourage teen labor and keep juveniles off the streets. Laws governing work in the home were rescinded altogether, and other regulations and enforcement were withdrawn. The rise of a work-force of immigrant labor created an underground resurgence of home labor. Furthermore, teen labor in general was encouraged by rising materialism, the idealization of work, and the laxity of the 1960s that had given young children greater independence. In the 1970s and 1980s, 63 percent of high school seniors and 42 percent of high school sophomores worked during the school year. The average employed teenager worked 20 hours a week for $275 a month.

Rising materialism, the relaxation of laws governing wage and hour regulation for child labor, along with the rise of the fast-food industry and its insatiable demand for workers sent the numbers of teenage workers soaring. Yet work in areas in which adolescents were hired was hard, repetitive, dull, dead-end, and did little or nothing to prepare teenagers for other trades or professions.

Ironically, it has been found that working has delayed the transition of adolescents into adulthood and has promoted rather than discouraged unacceptable behavior: smoking and the use of alcohol and drugs. Ellen Greenberger and Laurence Steinberg also found that teenagers who had jobs in the food industry and in stores usually developed a negative view of work (Greenberger and Steinberg).

In the three volumes discussed in this chapter, children have either chosen or been required to give up aspects of their childhood to take on responsibilities and activities that should belong to adults. In some cases, they work for money for a specific goal. In most cases, they have no choice but to work to bring income to the family. In a few cases, they work to hasten their stature as adults. But, contrary to folk wisdom, in only a few cases do teenagers find jobs that elevate them or prepare them for work as adults.

QUESTIONS AND PROJECTS

1. Conduct an interview with a teenager working in a fast-food restaurant. Prepare for it with a variety of questions about work place issues.
2. Conduct a survey of teen workers who are students in your school to determine how many work from need and how many work for spending money.
3. Write a comprehensive history of child labor in one industry: textiles, mining, farming, and so on.
4. Write a paper on a single child labor reformer.
5. Consider the problem of parents' work on their children. Gather information from printed sources and interviews.
6. Write an analysis of one of the short stories in Anne Mazer's *Working Days*.
7. Write a comparison and contrast between *The Grapes of Wrath* and *The Velvet Room*.
8. After research of various kinds, have a debate on the question of whether work is "good" or "bad" for teenagers.

FURTHER READING

Bartoletti, Susan C. *Kids on Strike*. Boston: Houghton Mifflin, 1999.

Bauer, Joan. *Hope Was Here*. New York: Penguin, 2000.

Cahn, Rhoda. *No Time for School, No Time for Play*. New York: J. Messner, 1972.

Clopper, Edward N. *Child Labor in City Streets*. New York: Macmillan, 1912.

Ehrenreich, Barbara. *Nickel and Dimed: On (Not) Getting By in America*. New York: Metropolitan Books, 2001.

Felt, J. P. *Hostages of Fortune*. Syracuse, NY: Syracuse University Press, 1965.

Freedman, Russell. *Kids at Work*. New York: Clarion Books, 1994.

Gay, Kathlyn. *Child Labor: A Global Crisis*. Brookfield, CT: Millbrook, 1998.

Greenberger, Ellen and Laurence Steinberg. *When Teenagers Work*. New York: Basic Books, 1986.

Greene, Laura. *Child Labor: Then and Now*. New York: F. Watts, 1992.

Gutman, Judith Mara. *Lewis W. Hine and the American Social Conscience*. New York: Walker and Company, 1967.

Hindman, Hugh D. *Child Labor: An American History*. Armonk, NY: M. E. Sharpe, 2002.

Jones, Carl. *Mind over Labor*. New York: Penguin, 1988.

Johnsen, Julia E. compiler. *Child Labor*. New York: H. W. Wilson, 1926.

Kielburger, Craig. *Free the Children*. New York: HarperCollins, 1998.

Levine, Marvin T. *Children for Hire*. Westport, CT: Praeger, 2003.

Mazer, Anne, ed. *Working Days*. New York: Persea Books, 1997.

Mofford, Juliet H., ed. *Child Labor in America*. Carlisle, MA: Discovery Enterprises, 1997.

Parker, David L. *Stolen Dreams*. Minneapolis, MN: Lerner Publications Co., 1998.

Rodgers, Gerry. *Child Work, Poverty and Underdevelopment*. Geneva, Switzerland: International Labour Office, 1981.

Schlosser, Eric. *Fast Food Nation*. Boston: Houghton Mifflin, 2001.

Schmitz, Cathryne L. *Child Labor*. Westport, CT: Greenwood Publications, 2004.

Snyder, Zilpha. *The Velvet Room*. New York: Atheneum, 1965.

Taylor, Ronald. *The Kid Business*. Boston: Houghton Mifflin Co., 1981.

———. *Sweatshop in the Sun*. Boston: Beacon Press, 1973.

Trattner, Walter I. *Crusade for the Children: A History of the National Child Labor Committee and Child Labor Reform in America*. New York: Quadrangle Books, 1970.

Vardinelli, Clark. *Child Labor and the Industrial Revolution*. Bloomington, IN: Indiana University Press, 1990

Whittaker, William. *Child Labor in America*. New York: Novinka Books, 2004.

Williams, Mary E., ed. *Child Labor and Sweat Shops*. San Diego, CA: Greenhaven Press, 1999

Selected Bibliography

Abbott, Edith. *Women in Industry*. New York: D. Appleton, 1910.

Applesbaum. Herbert. *Work in Market and Industrial Society*. Albany, NY: State University of New York Press, 1984.

Barnard, Robert. *Imagery and Theme in the Novels of Dickens*. Universitesforlaget: Norwegian University Press, 1974.

Bauer, Joan. *Hope Was Here*. New York: Penguin, 2000.

Baxter, Ralph H. *Sexual Harassment in the Work Place*. New York: Executive Enterprises Publications Co., 1981.

Bell, Daniel. *Work and Its Discontents: The Cult of Efficiency in America*. Boston: Beacon Press, 1956.

Bernstein, Irving. *Turbulent Years: A History of the American Worker, 1933–1941*. Boston: Houghton Mifflin, 1970.

Berthoff, Warner, ed. *Great Short Works of Herman Melville*. New York: Harper and Row, 1969.

Boyer, Richard O. and Herbert M. Morais. *Labor's Untold Story*. New York: United Electrical, Radio and Machine Workers of America, 1955.

Burnett, John, ed. *Annals of Labour*. Bloomington, IN: Indiana University Press, 1974.

Bushnell, Charles J. *The Social Problem at the Chicago Stock Yards*. Chicago: The University of Chicago Press, 1902.

Campbell, Helen. *Women Wage Earners*. Boston: Robert Bros., 1893.

Clarke, Elissa. *Stopping Sexual Harassment*. Detroit: Labor Education and Research Project, 1980

Clayton, Robert and David Roberts. *A History of England 1688 to the Present,* Vol II. Englewood Cliffs, NJ: Prentice-Hall, Inc., 1980.

Cochran, Thomas C. and William Miller. *The Age of Enterprise.* New York: Macmillan and Co., 1951.

Cole, G.D.H. and Raymond Postgate. *The Common People:1746–1946.* London: Methuen, 1938.

Davis, Rebecca Harding. *Life in the Iron Mills.* Ed. Tillie Olsen. Old Westbury, NY: The Feminist Press, 1972.

Dickens, Charles. *Hard Times.* New York: W. W. Norton and Company, 2001.

Ehrenreich, Barbara. *Nickel and Dimed: On (Not) Getting By in America.* New York: Metropolitan Books, 2001.

Feldman, Richard and Michael Betzold, eds. *End of the Line: Autoworkers of the American Dream.* New York: Weidenfeld and Nicolson, 1988.

Felt, J. P. *Hostages of Fortune.* Syracuse: Syracuse University Press, 1965.

Fogel, Richard Harter. *Melville's Shorter Tales.* Norman, OK: University of Oklahoma Press, 1960.

Foner, Philip S. *The Factory Girls.* Urbana, IL: University of Illinois Press, 1977.

———. *A History of the Labor Movement in the United States.* 4 vols. New York: International Publishers, 1947–1964.

Freedman, Russell. *Kids at Work.* New York: Clarion Books, 1994.

Fried, Albert. *Except to Walk Free: Documents and Notes in the History of American Labor.* New York: Anchor Books, 1974.

Glancy, Ruth. *A Student Companion to Charles Dickens.* Westport, CT: Greenwood Publishing, 1999.

Gutman, Herbert G. *Work, Culture, and Society in Industrializing America.* New York: Vintage, 1977.

Halevy, Elie. *History of the English People in the Nineteenth Century.* London: Benn, 1950.

Hall, Walter Phelps and Robert Albion. *A History of England and the British Empire.* Boston: Ginn and Company, 1946.

Halle, David. *America's Working Man.* Chicago: University of Chicago Press, 1984.

Heron, Alexander Richard. *Why Men Work.* New York: Arno Press, 1977.

Hobsbawm, E. J. *Industry and Empire.* London: Penguin Books, 1968.

Jamieson, Stuart. *Labor Unionism in American Agriculture.* Bulletin no. 326. Washington, DC: United States Labor Statistics, 1945.

Loftis, Anne. *Witness to the Struggle: Imagining the 1930s California Labor Movement.* Reno, NV: University of Nevada Press, 1998.

MacClean, Annie Marion. *Wage Earning Women*. New York: Macmillan, 1910.

Mazer, Anne, ed. *Working Days*. New York: Persea Books, 1997.

McTague, Michel J. *The Businessman in Literature*. New York: Philosophical Library, 1981.

McWilliams, Carey. *Factories in the Fields*. Boston: Little Brown, 1942.

Melville, Herman. "The Paradise of Bachelors and the Tartarus of Maids" in *Billy Budd, Sailor and Other Stories*. New York: Penguin Books, 1986.

———. *Bartleby the Scrivener. A Story of Wall Street*. New York: Simon and Schuster, 1997.

Mofford, Juliet H., ed. *Child Labor in America*. Carlisle, Mass.: Discovery Enterprises, 1997.

Moran, William. *The Belles of New England: The Women of the Textile Mills and the Families Whose Wealth They Wove*. New York: St. Martin's Press, 2002.

Orchard, B. G. *The Clerks of Liverpool*. Liverpool: J. Collinson, 1871.

Pessen, Edward. *Riches, Class, and Power Before the Civil War*. Lexington, MA: D.C. Heath and Company, 1973.

Pfaelzer, Jean. *Parlor Radical*. Pittsburgh: University of Pittsburgh Press, 1996.

Pike, E. Royston. *Hard Times: Human Documents of the Industrial Revolution*. New York: Praeger, 1966.

Plumb, J. H. *England in the Eighteenth Century*. Aylesbury, UK: Hunt Barnard and Co., 1950.

Rooke, Patrick. *The Age of Dickens*. London: Wayland, 1970.

Rose, Willie Lee, ed. *A Documentary History of Slavery in North America*. New York: Oxford University Press, 1976.

Santoro, Victor. *Fighting Back on the Job*. WA: Loompanics Unlimited, 1984.

Schlosser, Eric. *Fast Food Nation*. Boston: Houghton Mifflin, 2001.

Schmitz, Cathryne L. *Child Labor*. Westport, CT: Greenwood Publications, 2004.

Shannon, David A. *The Socialist Party of America*. New York: Macmillan, 1955.

Sheppard, Harold L., and Neal Q. Herrick. *Where Have All of the Robots Gone? Worker Dissatisfaction in the Seventies*. New York: The Free Press, 1972.

Shipler, David K. *The Working Poor*. New York: Alfred A. Knopf, 2005.

Sinclair, Upton. *The Jungle*. Introduction and Notes by Maura Spiegel. New York: Barnes and Noble, 2003.

Smith, Matthew. *Sunshine and Shadow*. Hartford, CT: J. B. Burr, 1869.

Snyder, Zilpha. *The Velvet Room*. New York: Atheneum, 1965.

Sprouse, Martin, ed. *Sabotage in the American Workplace*. San Francisco: Pressure Drop Press, 1992.

Stein, Walter. *California and the Dust Bowl Migration*. Westport, CT: Greenwood Press, 1973.

Steinbeck John. *The Grapes of Wrath*. New York: Penguin, 1976.

Stepto, Robert B. *From Behind the Veil: A Study of Afro-American Narrative*. Urbana, IL: University of Illinois Press, 1979.

Taylor, Paul S. *On the Ground in the Thirties*. Salt Lake City, UT: Peregrine Smith, 1983.

Terkel, Studs. *Working*. New York: Ballantine Books, 1972.

Vardinelli, Clark. *Child Labor and the Industrial Revolution*. Bloomington, IN: Indiana University Press, 1990

Watkins, T. H. *The Great Depression*. Boston: Little, Brown, 1993.

Wertheimer, Barbara Mayer. *We Were There: The Story of Working Women in America*. New York: Pantheon, 1977.

Whittaker, William. *Child Labor in America*. New York: Novinka Books, 2004.

Widick, B. J., ed. *Auto Work and Its Discontents*. Baltimore, MD: The Johns Hopkins University Press, 1976.

Wigginton, Eliot, ed. *Refuse to Stand Silently By*. New York: Doubleday, 1992.

Zimbalist, Andrew, ed. *Case Studies of the Labor Process*, New York: Monthly Review Press, 1979.

Zinn, Howard. *A People's History of the United States*. New York: HarperCollins, 1980.

Index

About the Author

CLAUDIA DURST JOHNSON is Professor Emeritus of English, University of Alabama. Her many books include *Understanding Melville's Short Fiction* (2005), *Youth Gangs in Literature* (2004), *Understanding The Odyssey* (2003), and *Daily Life in Colonial New England* (2002), all available from Greenwood Press.